LEXIPRO

ANGLAIS

BTS - IUT - DEUG
Formations tertiaires
Cadres d'entreprises

LES MOTS-CLÉS
DU TOURISME

Joëlle ROUANET-LAPLACE

Enseignante à la Faculté
de Sciences Economiques de Montpellier

éditions

1, rue de Rome 93561 Rosny cedex

© BREAL
Toute reproduction même partielle interdite
Dépôt légal : janvier 1993
ISBN : 2 85394 620 7
ISSN : 1159.3075

AVANT-PROPOS

Le présent glossaire appartient à une collection d'ouvrages terminologiques à l'intention des étudiants et des professionnels du secteur tertiaire.

Il s'adresse à tous ceux qui désirent acquérir ou perfectionner les notions fondamentales de l'anglais du tourisme.

Il convient tout particulièrement aux étudiants préparant l'épreuve d'anglais du BTS Tourisme - Loisirs.

Ce lexique, conçu avant tout comme un outil de travail, s'efforce de cerner les principaux problèmes afférents au tourisme et d'offrir au lecteur un panorama aussi complet que possible de la langue touristique.

Le vocabulaire sélectionné est présenté à partir du français, puis mis en contexte afin de permettre une meilleure assimilation et d'éviter tout contresens sur l'emploi de tel ou tel concept.

L'usage britannique (GB) et l'usage américain (US) sont indiqués chaque fois que cela est nécessaire.

Cet ouvrage ne prétend pas être exhaustif mais devrait fournir la base indispensable à une exploration plus approfondie des thèmes abordés.

L'auteur

DISPONIBLE DANS
LA COLLECTION
LEXIPRO

EN VENTE CHEZ
VOTRE LIBRAIRE

TABLE DES **M**ATIERES

AVANT PROPOS 3

ALPINISME ET SKI - Mountaineering and skiing 7

CLIMAT, TEMPS ET SAISONS - Climate, weather and seasons 12

HEBERGEMENT - Accommodation 16

    1. HOTELS - Hotel 16

        A. Catégories - Hotels types 16
        B. Chambres - Bedrooms, rooms 17
        C. Services et aménagement - Hotel services 18
        D. Formalités - Hotel formalities 18

    2. AUTRES TYPES D'HEBERGEMENT - Other types of accommodation 19

MER -Sea 23

THERMALISME - Health tourism 28

RESTAURATION - The catering industry 31

TOURISME D'AFFAIRES - Business tourism 35

    1. LES CONFERENCES - Conferences 37
    2. EQUIPEMENT POUR CONFERENCES - Conference facilities 38

TOURISME VERT - Green vacations 39

VILLES - Towns and cities 45

TRANSPORT - Transport, transportation 50
    1. TRANSPORT AERIEN - Air transport 50
    2. TRANSPORT FERROVIAIRE - Rail transport 55
    3. TRANSPORT MARITIME - Sea transport 58
    4. TRANSPORT ROUTIER - Road transport 61

FORMALITES (ASSURANCE, CHANGE, DOUANE, SANTE)
Formalities (insurance, exchange, customs, health) 64

INDUSTRIE TOURISTIQUE - Tourist trade 68

LISTE DES PRINCIPAUX PAYS ET DE LEURS HABITANTS 77

SIGNES PUBLICS - Public signs 83

CORRESPONDANCE - Letter-writing 84
    1. FORMULES D'INTRODUCTION - Opening salutations 84
    2. FORMULES DE POLITESSE - Closing salutations 84
    3. LISTE D'EXPRESSIONS STEREOTYPEES - Model sentences 84

LEXIQUE FRANÇAIS 86

LEXIQUE ANGLAIS 98

ALPINISME ET SKI
Mountaineering and skiing

■ **alpinisme**
mountaineering / mountain-climbing

alpiniste
mountaineer

alpin
alpine
This picturesque alpine resort, nestled in the valley, offers a variety of well-serviced ski-runs.

■ **altitude**
elevation
Yosemite Valley enjoys mild winters because of its 4000-foot elevation.

à 2000 mètres d'altitude
2000 metres above sea-level / above the level of the sea

mal des montagnes
altitude sickness

altipiste / altiport
snow runway / mountain landing strip

après-ski
after-ski
After-ski in Zermatt is very lively.

■ **avalanche**
avalanche / snowslide
Thanks to their training and experience, guides have the ability to assess a slope for avalanche risk or pick a safe route through a glacier's hidden crevasses.

couloir d'avalanche
avalanche gully

zone d'avalanche
avalanche area

bosse
mogul

brèche (montagne)
notch

canon (à neige)
snow cannons

cascade / chutes
cascade / falls / waterfalls
Nine hundred miles northeast of Buenos Aires, in the steamy tropical rain forests of Missione, the thundering falls of Iguazu form one of South America's greatest natural spectacles.

chaînes (véhicule)
chains / snow-chains

chalet
chalet

chasse-neige
snowplough

■ **col (montagne)**
pass / saddle
This pass is often impassable in winter.

crête
ridge

culminer
to soar / to tower
Much of the island is mountainous; the highest point, Mount Misery soars some 3, 792 feet into the tropical sky.

■ **descendre (pente)**
to go down a slope /
to plummet down a slope

dammer (piste) / dammé(e)
to groom / groomed
This resort offers 40 miles of groomed cross-country ski trails.

   machine à dammer
   snow-grooming machine

■ **domaine skiable**
ski area / ski field
Rising from 1600m to 2075m, Mount Hutt ranks as one of the highest ski fields in the southern hemisphere. The area has even been nicknamed "the ski field in the sky".

enneigement
snow conditions
Courchevel has a good history of snow conditions, but to cope with warm winters, it has a two-mile artificially created snow area.

■ **équipement (de ski)**
ski gear / ski equipment

   équipements (de la station)
   facilities
   On-field facilities include a ski school, a restaurant and a souvenir shop.

   équiper (s')
   to gear up
   Let's gear up for the slopes.

escalader
to climb
Climb up to that top! You'll have a breathtaking view of the valley.

   escalade
   mountain-climbing / rock-climbing

■ **étendre (s')**
to stretch
The Pyrenees are stretching from the Atlantic Ocean to the Mediterranean Sea, dividing France from Spain.

fixation (ski)
binding

   fixation avant / fixation arrière
   toe binding / heel binding

■ **forfait (ski)**
ski-pass
A five-day ski-pass is included in the overall price.

■ **funiculaire**
cable-car
In 1984, the 160-person fastest cable-car in the world was opened in Courchevel. It can carry 1900 skiers an hour up a 1700-metre run.

■ **glacier**
glacier

   ski sur glacier
   glacial skiing

   glaciaire
   glacial
   glacial lake, glacial valley....

glissement de terrain
landslide

■ **guide**
guide / mountain guide
Local guides know where to find excellent safe snow conditions surprisingly close to the beaten track.

hameau
hamlet
A secluded hamlet.

être héliporté
to be airlifted
They were airlifted to the glaciers.

■ **lac**
lake
Many beautiful glacial lakes dot the high country of Yosemite.
Several natural lakes, remnants of pre-historic Lake Lahontan that once covered most of northwestern Nevada, are set like blue jewels in the dry desert.

luge (sport)
luge / sled (US) / sledge / toboggan

    faire de la luge
    to luge / to sledge / to toboggan
    The children were tobogganing down the hill.

■ **moniteur de ski**
ski instructor
Qualified instructors will help you to perfect your technique and gain maximum pleasure from sport.

■ **montagne**
mountain
A visit to Georgia's mountains puts you knee-deep in beautiful scenery, pioneer history and genuine hospitality.

    montagnes couronnées de neige
    snow-capped mountains / snow-tipped mountains

    montagneux
    mountainous

    chaîne de montagnes
    mountain range
    The San Gabriel and San Bernardino mountain ranges rise abruptly to peaks over 10,000 feet, separating Los Angeles from desert lands to the north and forming an imposing backdrop for the teeming city.

These recreationally rich mountain ranges also offer a wealth of summer activities such as boating, hiking, parasailing and waterskiing.

motoneige
snowmobile

■ **neige**
snow / "white stuff"

    neige poudreuse
    powder snow / ungroomed snow / "cold smoke" (US)
    Skiers manœuver over a series of moguls that make skis chatter in spite of the deep cushion of powder snow.

    "soupe"
    slush

    neiges éternelles
    everlasting snow

névé
ice-field / snow field

■ **niché**
nestled
Spend a skiing holiday in Zermatt, one of the all-time great resorts, nestled below the Matterhorn.

parc national
national park
Renowned for its magnificent valley, great granite domes, peaks, waterfalls and giant sequoias, Yosemite National Park is a national treasure.

■ **paroi (rocheuse)**
cliff / wall

    paroi (de glace)
    ice-cliff

patinoire / patinage (sur glace)
ice rink, skating-rink / ice-skating

patiner
to skate
Skate on an outdoor ice rink with spectacular views of Half-Dome and Glacier Point.

■ **pente**
slope

pente douce / pente abrupte
gentle slope / steep slope

■ **pic**
peak / spitz

à pic (vu d'en bas)
steep

à pic (vu d'en haut)
sheer

un à-pic
bluff / sheer drop

■ **piste (ski alpin)**
chute / piste / slope / run
Every winter, millions of people around the world flock to slopes that were once the exclusive domain of the rich.

piste (ski de fond)
trail / track

raquette (montagne)
snowshoe
Join a park ranger on a walk into the woods on snowshoes.

■ **remonte-pente**
lift / ski lift / tow / ski-tow
Several tows will lift beginners to the easy runs.

refuge
mountain hut

rive
bank (river) / shore (lake)
Cabins dot the wooded shores of Big Bear Lake in the San Bernardino Mountains.

sauver
to rescue
Specially trained guides patrol glaciers rescuing injured or exhausted skiers.

sauvetage, sauveteur / équipe de sauvetage
rescue, rescuer / rescue team

■ **skier**
to ski / to take to the slopes
Take a helicopter ride to some remote spot to experience the exhilaration of skiing down virgin slopes.

ski (activité)
skiing
With developments in resort management, equipment, teaching methods and clothing, skiing has become a popular winter recreation.

ski alpin
alpine skiing / downhill skiing

ski de fond
cross-country skiing
If you have never tried cross-country skiing before, tuition is available at most ski schools and equipment can be hired cheaply.

ski de randonnée
ski touring

ski hors- piste
off-piste skiing
Many skiers yearn to venture off-piste and feel the thrill of carving their signature in fresh powder snow.

skieur / skieur débutant / skieur confirmé
skier / beginner / advanced skier
Courchevel boasts miles of runs to suit everyone, from the dedicated advanced skier right down to the beginner.

■ **sommet**
peak / summit / top
You will be airlifted to mountain tops by helicopter.

■ **sports d'hiver**
winter sports
Most of Nevada winter sports areas cluster around Lake Tahoe.

■ **station de ski**
ski resort / skiing resort / winter resort
Badger Pass -California's oldest ski resort - offers great downhill skiing.

■ **télésiège**
chair lift
Badger Pass is a modern ski resort with a triple chairlift, three double chairlifts, nine ski runs and a state-of-the-art fleet of snow-grooming machines.

■ **téléski**
skilift / T-bar
Ski lifts whisk skiers to heights otherwise accessible only by a day's climb.
One of this resort's greatest asset is a mind-blowing complex of lifts which have virtually eliminated the need to queue.

■ **traîneau**
sleigh
Visitors can board a horse-drawn sleigh for a ride through woods of spruce and fir past moose dipping their heads into a mountain stream.

promenade en traîneau
sleigh ride

torrent
stream / mountain stream
Mountain lakes and streams offer good catches all year, making the Shasta region an angler's paradise.

vaincre (un sommet)
to conquer (a peak)
Mountaineering means discovering new peaks to conquer.

■ **vallée**
valley
The Owens valley lies between California's two highest mountain ranges: the Sierra Nevada and White Mountains.

■ **vêtements de ski**
skiwear
High performance and high style skiwear is all the rage!

volcan
volcano (pl.: volcanoes)
The California Cascade range includes two gigantic glaciated volcanoes: the dormant 14162-foot Mount Shasta and the still active 10457-foot Mount Lassen.

volcan éteint /en activité
dormant /active volcano

CLIMAT, TEMPS ET SAISONS
Climate, weather and seasons

aube
dawn
"The rosy-fingered dawn".

> **à l'aube**
> at dawn / at daybreak

■ **baromètre**
barometer
Whatever the season, you consult the barometer to see what the weather is going to be like.

> **le temps est au beau fixe / variable / mauvais**
> the weather is set fair / changeable / bad

briller
to shine (sun) / to twinkle (stars)
He was staring at the stars twinkling in the sky.

■ **brouillard**
fog
Summer fog doesn't daunt the thousands of annual visitors who come to enjoy the charm and scenic beauty of Mendocino.

> **il y a du brouillard**
> it's foggy

> **brume**
> haze (légère) / mist

bruine
drizzle
Drizzle is very fine rain, almost like mist.

> **bruiner**
> to drizzle

calmer (se) (vent, tempête...)
to abate / to subside
The storm eventually abated.
The ship will remain in port until the storm subsides.

■ **chaleur**
warmth / heat (grande chaleur)

> **canicule**
> dog-days

> **vague de chaleur**
> heat-wave

■ **chuter (températures)**
to dip / to drop / to fall
If you must cross Death Valley in summer, make sure your car is in good condition and travel at night when temperatures drop.

■ **climat**
climate / clime
Southern California's main asset is its dry, subtropical climate.

■ **couvert (ciel)**
overcast
The grey overcast sky.

crépuscule
dusk / twilight

> **au crépuscule**
> at dusk / at twilight

doux (climat, températures)
mild
Coastal temperatures are generally mild year-round.

éclaircie
bright interval / sunny spell

s'eclaircir (ciel...)
to clear up
It has cleared up now! Let's go for a walk!

étouffant (chaleur)
stifling / sultry / sweltering
Though Redding and Red Bluff can be sweltering in midsummer, the region's plentiful lakes provide cooling retreats.

frais
cool / fresh
Pine forests, hidden lakes and cool air lure vacationers year-round to the San Bernardino range.

rafraichissant
cooling

se rafraîchir
to cool off
Sacramento sizzles in summer but residents and visitors cool off in the many lakes, rivers and mountain retreats nearby.

froid
cold

être transi de froid
to be chilled to the bone / to be numb with cold

gel / gelée
frost

gelée blanche
hoar frost

givre
glazed frost / ground frost

gelé (adj)
frozen
Brooks rivers and lakes are frozen to the delight of kids always fond of skating.

Il gèle à pierre fendre
it is freezing hard

grêle
hail

heure d'été
daylight saving time

humide
humid / moist / wet
Redwoods flourish in moist climates.

lune
moon

clair de lune
moonlight
Moonlight produces mirage effects and weird landscapes.

■ **météorologie**
meteorology

bulletin météorologique
weather report

prévisions météorologiques
weather forecast

mousson
monsoon / monsoon rains
The season in Southern Asia when there is a lot of heavy rain is called the monsoon

lever (se)
to arise (wind) / to lift (fog)

■ **neige / neiger**
snow / to snow

bulletin d'enneigement
snow report

chute de neige
snowfall
Many visitor attraction close in winter and heavy snowfall limits backroad driving.

coulée de neige
snowslide

nuage / nuageux
cloud / cloudy

■ **orage**
thunderstorm
A thunderstorm is brewing.

■ **ouragan**
hurricane
The Island is in the path of the hurricanes in the Caribbean.

■ **pluie / pleuvoir / pluvieux**
rain / to rain / rainy

le temps est à la pluie
it looks like rain

averse
rain-shower / shower

chute de pluie
downpour

giboulée
sudden shower

rafale
blizzard (snow) / gust (wind)

■ **saison**
season
The four seasons: spring, summer, autumn (fall, us), winter.

saison des pluies
rainy season

■ **sec / sécheresse**
dry / drought
Droughts, earthquakes, hurricanes are natural disasters.

■ **soleil**
sun

soleil de plomb
scorching sun

au lever du soleil / au coucher du soleil
at sunrise / at sunset

ensoleillé
sunny

gorgé de soleil / noyé de soleil
sun-drenched / sun-soaked
Hawaii's palm-fringed beaches are constantly sun-soaked and ventilated by light tradewinds

■ **température**
temperature
Death Valley has the dubious honour of having recorded America's highest temperature (134°F in july 1913).

tempéré
temperate

■ **tempête**
storm

tempête de neige
snowstorm

tempête de sable
sandstorm

être bloqué par une tempête
to be stormbound
The ferry was stormbound at Dover.

■ **temps**
weather
California's biggest asset might be its weather: lots of sun, little rain and low humidity make it possible to enjoy outdoor activities the year round.

quel temps fait-il ?
what's the weather like ?

typhon
typhoon
A typhoon sank a sailing-boat in the Pacific Ocean, drowning 8 people.

■ **vent**

wind

The wind is dying away.

alizé

trade-wind / tradewind

The Caribbean, located between the Equator and the Tropic of Cancer, enjoy warm sunshine tempered by light tradewinds for the greater part

of the year.

bourrasque

squall

grand vent

high wind

vent doux

gentle breeze

HEBERGEMENT
Accommodation

■ **hébergement**
accommodation / lodging (US)
This hotel is ideal for guests looking for an elegant accommodation at a reasonable place right in the centre of London.
All lodging within the park on the South Rim of the Grand Canyon is provided by Grand Canyon National Park Lodges.

héberger
to put up
Small farmers in Italy are making ends meet by putting up guests.

hébergement en demi-pension
half-board accommodation / modified American plan.

hébergement en pension complète
full-board accommodation / American plan

capacité d'hebergement
accommodation capacity

1
HOTELS
hotels

■ **hôtel**
hotel
Conferences, wedding facilities, golf holiday are the speciality of this old-established hotel.

■ **hôtelier (n)**
hotelier / hotel-keeper

Europe's hoteliers experienced a difficult year in 1990.

hôtelier (adj.)
hotel
hotel amenities / hotel capacity ...

chaîne hôtelière
hotel chain
Most hotel chains cluster around airports or in main cities.

résidence hôtelière
aparthotel / serviced apartments
Increasingly, in recent years, the busy executive has turned to serviced apartments in preference to hotels.

zone hôtelière
hotel strip

■ **tenir un hôtel**
to manage a hotel / to run a hotel
This pleasant hotel is most efficiently run by a charming couple.
A family-run hotel.

##
CATEGORIES
hotel types
---

hôtel classe touriste
tourist class hotel
The tourist class hotels we have carefully selected represent excellent value.

hôtel de luxe
de-luxe hotel / luxury hotel

hôtel quatre étoiles
four -star hotel (official rating: four stars)

─────── ───────

CHAMBRES
bedrooms, rooms

■ **chambre**
bedroom / room
The bedroooms are all interior designed in English country-house style with marble bathrooms.
All the rooms and en-suite facilities have been totally renovated and refurbished with great care.

chambre avec bains
room with private bath / room with bathroom en-suite

chambre climatisée
air-conditioned room

chambre communicante / chambre voisine
connecting room / adjoining room

chambre pour deux personnes
double room / double-bedded room / twin room / twin-bedded room (lits jumeaux)

chambre individuelle
single room
The hotel has recently been totally interior designed and refurbished to a very high specification and offers 42 rooms-singles, twins, doubles-each with en-suite bath.

chambre avec vue
room with a view

suite / suite de luxe / petite suite
suite / luxury, penthouse suite / junior suite
Our luxury suites have woodburning fireplaces and private ocean-view decks.

■ **bien-aménagé / bien-équipé**
well-appointed / well equipped, appointed (with) / equipped (with)
All the rooms are superbly appointed affording the ultimate comfort.
A well-equipped country hotel.
A country inn equipped with all modern amenities.

calme (adj.)
calm / peaceful / quiet / tranquil / serene
Paddington is a quiet residential area-its streets reflecting the prosperous Empire days.

■ **confort / confortable**
comfort / comfortable
Having every amenity and the last word in comfort, this manor house is the perfect place for a rest.

■ **donner (sur)**
to overlook / to command a view on, over
The meals are served in our spacious dining-room commanding a sweeping view over the lake.
This hotel overlooks the charming little town of Etretat and enjoys spectacular views over the famous cliffs and the coastline.

meublé / meubles
furnished / furniture (sg.: a piece of furniture)
The rooms are pleasantly furnished in antique style.

SERVICES ET AMÉNAGEMENT
hotel services

aménagements pour les handicapés
facilities for the disabled / facilities for the handicapped / wheel-chair access

ascenseur
elevator(US) / lift

change
currency exchange

garde d'enfants
baby-sitting service

navette gratuite
courtesy coach / courtesy shuttle

parking
car-park / garage facilities / parking facilities
Two car-parks are within walking distance of the hotel.
Parking facilities are available to all guests.

FORMALITÉS
hotel formalities

■ **annulation / annuler**
cancellation / to cancel
A two-day cancellation policy.

Cancellations have to be made before 6p.m. on the arrival date.

frais d'annulation
cancellation fees

■ **arrhes**
deposit
A deposit of £150 or 20 % of the total cost-whichever is the greater-must be enclosed with this form to secure your booking.

verser des arrhes
to make a deposit payment / to pay a deposit
Deposit payments should be made at least two months prior to departure date.

bon d'échange / bon de paiement
voucher
If your booking is guaranteed by a voucher, you pay for the room in advance and present the voucher on arrival.

bon de paiement émis par une ligne aérienne (MCO)
Miscellaneous Order / Service Order

■ **complet**
fully booked / no vacancy / no vacancies
I'm afraid we're fully booked this week-end.
Sorry, no vacancies!

■ **descendre (dans un hôtel)**
to check in
She checked in at the Chelsea Hotel.

■ **enregistrement / enregistrer**
check-in / registration / to check in / to register
Guests must check in at the front desk.

fiche (à remplir)
registration card / registration form

Would you fill in this registration form?
A registration card is used to record the full name, nationality, home address and signature of each guest.

heure d'arrivée / heure de départ
check-in time / check-out time

■ **libre (chambre) / libérer (une chambre)**
vacancy / vacancies / to vacate (a room)
It is standard practice for hoteliers to require that guests vacate their rooms by noon.

numéro vert
freephone number / toll-free number
1-800 numbers are toll-free numbers in the USA.
Dial toll-free 1-800-228-2028 to make a reservation.

■ **quitter (un hôtel)**
to check out
He checked out of the hotel this morning.

départ de l'hôtel, remise des clés
check-out
Express check-out... Goodbye at the drop of a key... Another reflection of our legendary dedication to service!

■ **réservation**
booking / reservation
We have much pleasure in confirming your booking of two single rooms with baths.

réservation en bloc
block-booking

réservation par téléphone / par telex
telephone-booking /
telex-booking

système de réservations électronique
computer reservation system (C.R.S.)

tableau de réservations
reservation chart

éffectuer une réservation / réserver
to make a booking / to make a reservation / to book / to reserve
I'd like to book a twin-bedded room from the 21st of september to the morning of the 26th.

■ **taux d'occupation (d'un hôtel)**
occupancy rate
Hoteliers try to increase the occupancy rate by offering holidaymakers rock-bottom prices in the low season.

afficher (un taux d'occupation de ..)
to post an occupancy rate of...
Corsican hotels posted an occupancy rate of 80% last summer.

taxe de séjour
residence tax (US) / sejourn tax

2
AUTRES TYPES D'HEBERGEMENT
other types of accommodation

■ **appartement**
flat / apartment (US)
Your apartment will only be a few steps away from the finest shops, restaurants and neighbourhood conveniences.

échange d'appartement
flat swap

meublé
furnished apartment, furnished flat / self-catering flat

We offer you a large selection of stylish furnished apartments in elegantly restored Victorian homes.

■ **auberge**
inn

Set on a hillside, overlooking the vineyards, this charming inn will enchant every visitor.

■ **auberge de jeunesse**
hostel / youth hostel / community hotel (cotel, US)

They travelled through Europe, always staying in youth hostels.
Hostels provide travellers of all ages an inexpensive, friendly atmosphere for spending the night.

"Café- Couette " / chambre d'hôte
"Bed and Breakfast"

Part of the charm of B&Bs is the chance they offer visitors to learn about the area from their host and other guests; it's a good way to exchange ideas on activities, restaurants and "must sees".

■ **camping (activité) / faire du camping**
camping / to go camping

Camping is not permitted along roasides, parking lots or day-use only areas.
The US Virgin Islands offer superlative camping on the stunning white-sand beaches.

terrain de camping
campsite / campground (US)

Campsites are usually serviced by a cafeteria, convenience stores and showers in separate buildings.
Death Valley National Monument operates 9 campgrounds throughout the monument.

camping-car
camper / motorhome / recreational vehicle (R.V.) / van

Buy a recreational vehicle and you'll enjoy the lifestyle of the semi-nomad.
Vans come equipped with sleeping quarters, stove and refrigerator.

camping sauvage
free camping / rough camping (ant.: supervised camping)

caution
secutity bond / security deposit

A refundable security deposit will be required; it will serve as a guarantee regarding any damages and cost of telephone calls.

chalet
chalet

Designed to take full advantage of the spectacular view over Lake Wakatipu, this comfortable chalet boasts a large stone fireplace.

■ **château**
castle / chateau (pl.: eaus/eaux)

The chateaux of the Loire Valley built during the reign of Charles VIII, in a region of outstanding natural beauty, this chateau has been turned into a hotel of great distinction.
Perched on a hilltop, this secluded castle commands breathtaking views over the valley.

chaumière
thatched cottage

A cluster of grey thatched cottages set against a thickly wooded hillside makes this part of Buckland-in-the-Moor one of the most photographed corners of England.

■ **cottage**
cottage

Try our idyllic hideaway and unique vacation resort of de luxe cottages set on a private island in the Caribbean Sea.

demeure de caractère
mansion
Secluded in its own park, this mansion will make you revive and appreciate the special charm of the past.

■ ferme
farm / farmhouse
This farmhouse provides an attractive base for visitors who value fresh flowers, informality and quiet domestic efficiency.

logis à la ferme
farmhouse accommodation

vacances à la ferme
farm holidays

■ gîte (rural, de montagne)
lodge
Rustic cabins and lodges, secluded campsites provide a choice of overnight accommodation in Yosemite national park.

le gîte et le couvert
board and lodging / room and board

■ hostellerie
country house hotel / hostelry (US)
Built of local pink granite and typifying the style of architecture found on the island of Jersey, the Little Grove is a country house hotel with traditional values and service.

■ louer
to hire / to rent
To rent holiday accommodation. They rented a luxury serviced apartment with all of London in easy reach.

agence de location
rental agency

manoir
manor house
Southern England has its share of stately homes, but its greatest architectural wealth lies in the manor houses.

■ motel
motel / motorlodge
In this family-owned motel, you can be assured of a friendly and personalized service.

■ multi-propriété
time-sharing
Time-sharing is a system of part ownership of a property.

appartement en multi-propriété
time-share

acheter en multi-propriété
to buy (a flat, a house...) on a time-sharing basis

■ pension (de famille)
guest house

pensionnaire / hôte payant
paying guest

ranch
ranch
No holiday captures the spirit of America so completely as a stay on a western ranch.

séjour dans un ranch
ranching / ranch holiday
For the very best of western adventures, try ranching!

relais
country inn / countryside inn

répertorier
to list
The National Association of Agritourism lists 1,5000 farms offering hospitality from the

Alto Adige to Sicily, and it estimates that there are at least 5,000 others that go unlisted.

repertorié

listed (ant.: unlisted)

situé

located / set / situated

This two-bedroom flat is conveniently located in the centre of the London West End.

MER
Sea

■ **abriter (de)**
to shelter (from)
The high promontory that shelters San Diego Bay from the Pacific Ocean offers great harbour views.
The Elephant and Cardamom Hills have always sheltered the narrow coastal state of Kerala from the rest of India.

abrité
sheltered
Ventnor, sheltered from the north by the huge mass of Saint Boniface Down, is one of the warmest holiday resorts on the island.

algues
seaweed

■ **aménagement du littoral**
coastal development / shore development
The 25-mile stetch of barrier reef from Kitty Hawk to Corolla is the latest hot spot in coastal development in North Carolina.

anse
cove

archipel
archipelago
The Philippine archipelago.

atoll
atoll
Life on remote atolls continues to fascinate and inspire writers.

baie
bay
Water-taxis shuttle pedestrians around the bay, making stops at major waterfront hotels.

■ **bains de mer**
bathing / sea bathing
Brembridge is a quiet seaside village with good bathing and wide firm sands at low tide.

bains de soleil
sunbathing

■ **bateau (fond transparent)**
glass-bottom boat
Glass-bottom boat trips explore the colourful undersea marine life and vegetation of the island's legendary clear waters.

■ **bordé (de)**
fringed (with) / lined (with)

plage bordée de palmiers
palm-fringed beach / beach lined with palm-trees

brisants
breakers / surf

■ **bronzer**
to get a suntan / to sunbathe

crème à bronzer
suntan lotion / suntan oil

cabotage
coasting / coastal navigation

cocotier
coconut

> **cocoteraie**
> coconut grove
> *Beautiful coconut groves line this paradise island.*

coquillages
seashells / shells
Waterfront stores sell souvenirs ranging from seashells, jewelry and T-shirts to model ships.

corail
coral
Divers explore coral canyons, caves and ledges, viewing a variety of coral.

■ **côte**
coast
Big Sur is one of California's most spectacular stretches of coast.

> **côtier**
> coastal
> *Fort Point -the brick and granite coastal fortification underneath the Golden Gate Bridge- is open daily for tours.*
> *The coastal state of Kerala is lush and unspoiled.*

crique
creek

crustacés
shellfish

■ **déchiquetée (côte)**
rugged
Much of the island is uninhabited with a great deal of its rugged coastline only accessible by sea.

découpée (côte)
indented
Half-day bus tours transport visitors to the island's indented coastline for a look at scenery and wildlife.

dune
dune

émaillé (de) / parsemé (de)
dotted (with)
Coastal areas are dotted with beaches and sea-sculpted rock formations.

■ **ensoleillé**
sunny
All the main villages lie on the island's sunny west coast.

> **coin très ensoleillé**
> suntrap

> **noyé de soleil**
> sun-baked / sun-drenched / sun-soaked
> *Fiji's main attractions are mountains, tropical forests, sun-drenched beaches, palm-fringed lagoons and coral reef.*

entourer
to ring / to surround
Explore the lush tropical Lost Islands Jungle surrounding mangrove islands and tide pools home to native fish, crocodiles, birds ans sea turtles.

> **entouré (de)**
> ringed (by) / surrounded (by)
> *Just off the Kerala coast are the tiny islands of the Lakshadweep chain, ringed by unexplored reefs which are teeming with underwater life.*

■ **étendue (n)**
stretch
The long stretches of sand and water from Santa Monica to Long Beach are dotted with fishing piers and marinas.

■ **falaise**
cliff

Along the north coast of Devon, promontories of grey rock alternate with sheer, tall cliffs and long stretches of sand.

front de mer
ocean-front / sea- front / waterfront

San Francisco's waterfront is its chief drawing card. Attractions around Fisherman's Wharf and Pier 39 draw most visitors.
Papeete is delightfully provincial and designed for leisurely wandering along the sea-front, sipping coffee in a sidewalk cafe or visiting art galleries.

■ fruits de mer
seafood

Specialties at seafood restaurants include fresh crab, lobster, prawns and "cioppino"-the heroic shellfish stew you dip into with your fingers.

grotte
cave / cavern / grotto

Magnificent artistry can be seen at the Ajanta caves.
On the wild north coast of Sutherland, a vast cavern cuts into a limestone cliff.

■ île
island

The Caribbean Sea is studded with islands.
Fiji: a tropical group of islands lapped by the warm waters of the South Pacific providing everything needed for a perfect holiday.

les îles Britanniques
the British Isles

îlot
islet

iode
iodine

jetée
pier

The fishing pier is organized for round-the-clock angling.
You can fish from the pier with a licence and buy bait and tackle.

lagon
lagoon

■ (le) large (n)
(the) open sea

au large (des côtes françaises)
off (the French coast)

■ littoral
coastline / shoreline

This scenic road offers fine views along the shoreline.

proche du littoral (île)
offshore (island)

Santa Catalina Island -California's only offshore resort- has lured local pleasure-seekers since the 1890s.

marée
tide

à marée basse / à marée haute
at low tide / at high tide

Caves can be explored at low tide.

le flux et le reflux
ebb and flow

marin (adj.)
marine (adj.)

True to the city's marine tradition, the port of Miami is the busiest cruise port in the world.

marin (n.c.)
sailor

marin d'eau douce
landlubber

■ **mer**
sea

> **mer agitée / démontée / grosse / moutonneuse**
> rough / raging / heavy / choppy sea
>
> **mer étale**
> smooth sea
>
> **en mer**
> at sea
>
> **nautisme**
> sailing / yachting

palmier
palm / palm-tree

> **palmeraie**
> palm grove

parasol
umbrella

pêcheur
fisherman

> **village de pêcheurs**
> fishing village
>
> *Polperro has all that a Cornish fishing village is supposed to have lime-washed houses around a small harbour, narrow streets, tales of smugglers and a timeless sense of peace.*
>
> **pêcher**
> to fish
>
> **pêche / pêche sous-marine**
> fishing / spear fishing

■ **phare**
lighthouse
Saint Catherine lighthouse warns shipping in the Channel of the coastline's dangers.

■ **plage**
beach

> **plage de sable, de galets**
> sandy beach / pebbly beach, shingle beach
>
> *This four-mile stretch of windswept sandy beach is a dramatic place to hike-though unsafe for swimming.*
> *The mile-long shingle beach at Seaton sweeps from high cliffs in the west to the mouth of the Axe in the east.*

■ **plonger (gén.) / plonger (avec bouteilles) / plonger (sans bouteilles)**
to dive / to scuba-dive / to skin-dive (= to snorkel)

> **plongée**
> diving / skin-diving / snorkeling
>
> *The coral-studdied Florida keys is today's coluorful underwater environment for thousands of skin and scuba-diving enthusiasts.*

■ **port**
harbour
San Diego's beautiful harbour offers parks for strolling, piers and embankments for fishing, boat-launching facilities and lots of places to watch the ships go by.

> **port de pêche**
> fishing harbour
>
> **port de plaisance**
> marina / recreational boat harbour / yachting harbour
>
> *When you see the masts of Marina Del Rey, it's easy to believe that this man-made recreational boat harbour is the world's largest.*

poste de secours
first-aid hut

■ **presqu'île**
peninsula
Pristine beaches, surf crashing against craggy rocks and wave-warped cypresses have made the Monterey Peninsula famous around the world.

■ **promontoire**
headland / promontory
"Strange, introverted and storm-twisted beauty"- so the poet Robinson Jeffers described Point Lobos, the promontory jutting into the Pacific south of Carmel.

récif
reef
South Molle Island is surrounded by fringing reefs and consists of 1000 acres of shrub and forest with many inlets, bays coral gardens and reefs.

■ **rivage**
shore
Since sailors were first shipwrecked on faraway shores, remote islands have always held a fascination.

■ **situé (être)**
to lie / to be located / to be set / to be situated
Between Hispaniola and the Virgin Islands lie Puerto Rico, a bustling picturesque member of the American Commonwealth.

■ **soleil**
sun / sunshine
paresser au soleil
to bask in the sun / to laze in the sun / to soak up the sun
She enjoyed soaking up the sun sipping an exotic cocktail.

sports nautiques
aquatic sports / watersports

Watersports: sailing, scubadiving, skindiving, snorkelling, surfing, windsurfing, water skiing, yachting...

■ **surplomber**
to overlook (something) / to jut above/over (something)
Perched on a hill overlooking the coast, this restaurant is a favourite watering hole for locals and tourists.
A volcanic mountain range jutting above the Atlantic off the coast of Morocco, Madeira is a tropical Eden.

■ **station balnéaire**
sea resort / seaside resort
Honolulu: an ideal seaside resort for those wanting golden sands !
Hastings is a popular seaside resort with a unique blend of old and new.

station classée
classified resort

sous-marin (adj.)
underwater
The underwater flora

vague
wave

vent
wind
exposé au vent
windy / windswept

■ **vierge (intact, pas défiguré)**
unspoilt / unspoiled
St. Lucia, an island of rare contrasts, achieves a perfect balance between modern resorts custom-built for tourists and unspoilt villages

voilier
sailing-boat

27

THERMALISME
Health tourism

■ affection
affliction / ailment / trouble

affection cardiaque
cardiac troubles

affection digestive
digestive ailment

affection hépatique
liver ailment

affection rénale
kidney ailment

affection rhumatismale
rheumatic affliction

■ bain
bath

bain d'algues
algae bath / seaweedy treatment

bain de boue
mudbath

In Calistoga, a spa-town situated at the foot of Mount Helena, thousands of tourists slither into mudbaths and slide into mineral pools.

bain de vapeur
steambath

■ bains (établissement)
baths

The Roman baths were a social centre; in addition to cleansing one's body one could take exercise, relax or read.

■ balneothérapie
balneotherapy

cure
cure / thermal cure

A cure is not always a sinecure!
This extremely luxurious and futuristic spa offers all the facilities for a thermal cure.
Thermal cures stimulate recuperative powers and accelerate recovery.

cure d'amaigrissement
slimming course / weight-loss programme

Weight-loss programmes are administered under nutritional supervision.

cure de remise en forme
fitness cure

faire une cure
to take a cure / to take the waters

■ curiste
cure-taker / spa-goer

Healthy, pure and natural, this environment offers cure-takers an ideal setting for a regenerative rest.

curatif
curative / healing

Curative properties, healing virtues, healing waters...

diététicien / diététique (science) / diététique (adj.)
dietitian / dietetics / dietetic

diurétique
diuretic
Diuretic qualities.

■ **forme (être en)**
to be fit / to be in shape / to be in trim
He felt relaxed and fit after his holiday. Why not try thalassotherapy? It will put you in trim!

garder la forme
to keep fit

en pleine forme
as fit as a fiddle

■ **guérir**
to cure / to heal
Thermal treatments do not cure at once, but they allow a reduction in medicine consumption.

massage / masseur
massage / masseur
The treatment consists of spray-showers, steambaths and massages.

nutrition / nutritioniste
nutrition / nutritionist

obèse
obese / overweight

obésité
obesity

piscine
pool
The open-air pools are fed by a radioactive thermal spring which flows at a constant temperature.

■ **prévention**
prevention
Oligo-mineral waters are most commonly used for the prevention and cure of kidney stones.

prévenir
to prevent

préventif
preventive / preventative

régime
diet
The Kneipp cure, practised in German spas, consists of hydrotherapy, exercise, diet and relaxation.

suivre un régime
to be on a diet

régime équilibré
balanced diet

■ **repos**
relaxation / rest
This spa is a peaceful oasis devoted to rest and relaxation.

se reposer
to relax / to rest

■ **revitalisant**
rejuvenating
You can drink our rejuvenating spa-water and take a bath in it every morning.

revitaliser
to rejuvenate

■ **sain**
healthy
A healthy climate.

santé
health
What better use of leisure than to improve one's health?

en bonne santé
healthy (ant.: unhealthy)

sauna
sauna

■ **soulager**
to relieve
Mudbaths relieve pain and fatigue and are used in treatments for rheumatic diseases.

soulagement
relief
Used in drinks and inhalations, the waters of Mont Dore give immediate relief to the cure-takers.

■ **source**
spa / spring
Hot volcanic springs, mineral springs, thermal springs...
The gushing springs of Desert Hot Springs -which can reach temperatures of 207°F- are cooled to under 110°F for therapeutic and recreational uses.

■ **station climatique**
health resort

■ **station thermale**
spa / spa-town / thermal resort
Châtel-Guyon is the most important spa-town in Europe for the digestive system.

■ **thérapeutique (adj.) / thérapie**
therapeutic / therapy
The therapeutic virtues of the waters are complemented by the appropriate thermal equipment and by modern methods.

crénothérapie
crenotherapy

fangothérapie
fangotherapy

hydrothérapie
hydrotherapy
The undisputable and scientifically proven benefits of hydrotherapy.

thalassothérapie
thalassotherapy

thermal
thermal
Nieuweschans, a charming fortified village, is both an international thermal spa and a modern thermal complex.

thermes
thermae
Evian's thermae are one of the best places to cure liver and stomach troubles.

■ **traitement**
treatment
These waters are particularly recommended for the treatment of metabolic ailments.

traiter
to treat
To treat arthritis, the spa of Royat has perfected an amazing therapy based on the use of thermal gas, either alone or associated with mineral water.

RESTAURATION
The catering industry

■ **addition**
bill / check(US) / tab(US)
Could we have the bill please?

> **payer l'addition**
> to foot the bill / to pay the bill

amuse-gueule
appetizer
A new expanded menu offers a large assortment of appetizers including crabmeat cocktail, shrimps and oysters.

■ **auberge**
inn / country inn
We stopped at a cosy inn, specialising in Irish stew, Celtic steaks and fresh seafood.

> **aubergiste**
> innkeeper

■ **bar**
public bar / pub
The tradition of games like darts is largely retained in British pubs.
The social hub of Irish life is the pub, with its own unique charm.

> **bar à vins**
> wine-bar

■ **boissons**
beverages / drinks
Drinks are served in the cosy lounge.

> **boissons alcoolisées**
> alcoholic drinks

> **boissons non alcoolisées**
> soft drinks

> **boissons gazeuzes**
> carbonated drinks, fizzy drinks

cadre
setting
Coconut Grove, Florida, is the perfect setting for this charming restaurant where you will enjoy intimate dining on the romantic terrace.

■ **carte**
à la carte menu / menu
What's on the menu?

> **carte des vins**
> wine-list
> *Would you like to see the wine-list Sir?*
> *Draught beer is available plus a very adequate wine list of local dry white wines as well as imported selections.*

> **manger à la carte**
> to eat à la carte

client
customer / diner (restaurant) / guest / patron (pub)
Diners can watch their specialties being prepared in ovens, broilers or deep-fryers by skilled chefs.

■ **commande / commander**
order / to order
Are you ready to order? Can I take your order?
In pubs, last orders are usually around 11p.m.

■ **cuisine (art culinaire)**
cuisine
Enjoy a variety of dining options: fine dining offering award-winning French cuisine, Californian cuisine in a romantic

setting or exquisite Italian cuisine in an informal atmosphere.

cuisiner
to cook

cuisinier / chef cuisinier
cook / chef

dessert
dessert / pudding
For dessert, try the Key Lime Pie.

■ **étoile**
star
Three stars are given to top-rate restaurants where only the very best food is available.

■ **gastronomie**
gastronomy

gastronome / gastronomique
gastronome / gasronomic

guide gastronomique
good food guide / dining guide / restaurant directory
Free dining guides preview restaurants in major southern Californian cities.

■ **goûter / déguster**
to sample / to taste / to try
Try one of the Shannon-area castles, where medieval banquets allow visitors to sample life in the 15th century.
The hospitality room is located on the top floor of the Chateau where wines may be sampled and purchased.

grill (établissement)
grill / steak-house
The Spyglass Grill is a great spot for a snack while claiming a bird's-eye view of the 9th green of Spyglass Hill Golf Course.

hors-d'œuvre
hors-d'œuvre / starter
Smoked salmon pâté is a traditional Irish starter.

■ **inviter (quelqu'un au restaurant)**
to wine and dine (someone)

■ **menu (à prix fixe)**
table d'hôte menu / set meal / set menu
Not all restaurants have a table d'hôte as well as an à la carte menu. Check when booking.

avec menu fixe
on a table d'hôte basis

■ **nourriture**
fare / food / grub (coll)
Along with trendy eateries and more traditional European dining spots, San Francisco abounds in restaurants spotlighting Pacific Rim and other lesser-known fares.
Try the China Moon Cafe: bare-bones atmosphere but fine spicy food!

plat (récipient, mets) / plat (partie du repas)
dish / course (ex.: a three-course dinner)

plat à emporter
food to take-away / food to take out (US) / take-away food (ant.: food to eat in)

plat du jour / suggestion du jour
the daily special, today's special
Ask about our daily special!

■ **pourboire**
gratuity / tip
In some establishments tip is included in bills as a service charge. Check to be sure!

laisser un pourboire
to give a tip / to tip
If there is a service charge, you are not expected to tip as well, unless, of course, you want to.

proposer
to feature
Many restaurants feature an early bird special menu.
The menu features international as well as American specialties.

■ **recommander**
to recommend

recommandé
recommended
This country inn is highly recommended and much praised by all guests.

renommé / reputé
celebrated / famed / famous / renowned / well-known

■ **repas**
meals
Buffet breakfast, à la carte meals and drinks are served on the terrace overlooking the lake.

petit-déjeuner (anglais, continental...)
breakfast (full English breakfast, continental breakfast) / brunch (breakfast + lunch on Sundays, at 11a.m.)

déjeuner
lunch

dîner / souper
dinner / supper

■ **réserver (une table)**
to book (a table)
I would like to book a table for a party of five (for five).

■ **restaurant**
eatery (US) / eating place (US) / dining spot / restaurant
San Francisco's 3, 300 restaurants offer every kind of dining, from haute cuisine to family-style meals.

restaurateur
restaurant manager / restaurant owner

restaurer (se)
to have something to eat

restauration rapide
fast food

aller au restaurant
to dine out / to eat out / to go out wining and dining / to have a meal out
Dining out in Dublin is a popular past-time, so to avoid disappointment, book a table well in advance.

salon de thé
coffee-shop / tea-shop
The hotel has a coffee-shop on the ground-floor where beverages and snacks are served all day.

■ **service**
service
Is service included?
Service is fast and courteous and the atmosphere pleasant.

service de premier ordre
service is second to none

serveur / serveuse
waiter / waitress

aide-serveur
busboy (US)

servir
to serve
Breakfast is served in the rooms or in the garden.

■ **sommelier**
wine-waiter

■ **spécialité**
speciality / speciality dish
Try our Turkish specialities!

table d'hôte
table d'hôte / set meal service

T.V.A.
V.A.T. (value added tax)

■ **vin (blanc, pétillant, rosé, rouge...)**
wine (white, sparkling, rosé, red...)

    cave (de negociant-éleveur)
    winery / winery-estate
    Beringer, Christian Brothers and Charles Krug, three romantic

wineries offer complimentary tours and tastings.

dégustation de vins
wine-tasting

grand cru, vin millésimé
vintage wine

(à) volonté
unlimited
unlimited beer / unlimited wine...

    nourriture à volonté
    all-you-can-eat (US)
    On Fridays, try our all-you-can-eat buffet!

■ affaires
business

centre d'affaires
business centre
The European Quality Alliance is planning to open fully equipped business centres throughout Eastern Europe.

classe Affaires
business class / Executive class
Business class passengers receive all the time-and-hassle-saving advantages of privileged check-in and priority baggage handling.

homme d'affaires
businessman

homme en voyage d'affaires
business traveller
Hotels are investing heavily in new technology aimed at improving and simplifying the stay of the business traveller.

rendez-vous d'affaires
business appointment
Fax machines and such amenities as chauffeur-driven limousines for business appointments are examples of the Ritz's aim of running a few years ahead of the competition in hotel services.

voyages d'affaires (sens géneral)
business travel (unc) / executive travel
Business travel has gained a high degree of importance in the late eighties. The Tapei International Convention Centre is sure to put Taiwan more firmly on the international business travel map.

voyage d'affaires
business trip

voyager pour affaires
to go on a business trip / to make a business trip / to travel on business
When travelling on business, you won't fail to appreciate a comfortable lounge providing business facilities.

■ cadre
executive
Madrid's Ritz Hotel at the hub of the Spanish capital provides a favourite stopover for executives.

■ contrat
contract / deal
The company won a contract to build 50 planes.

conclure un contrat
to clinch a deal / to strike a deal
He was in Hungary, trying to clinch a deal for his employer.

délégué
delegate / representative
All the different branches of the union elect delegates to the annual conference.

■ durer
to last
The International Conference on Urban Life will last five days.

■ équipement (services, confort)
amenities

équipement (infrastructure)
facilities
There are extensive conference facilities at the hotel including four large conference rooms and eight function rooms.

■ **frais (n)**
expenses / fees

frais d'annulation / frais de déplacement / frais d'inscription (congrès)
cancellation fees / travelling expenses / registration fees (convention)

couvrir (frais, dépenses)
to cover (expenses)
The local and travelling expenses will be covered by the company.

■ **inscription**
registration

bulletin d'inscription / formulaire d'inscription
registration form
Please fill in the registration form and send it back to the organizing committee at your earliest convenience.

s'inscrire
to register

lieu
venue
Selecting the venue for a conference is more and more governed by the proximity of golfing facilities.

■ **avoir lieu**
to be held / to take place
The next International Symposium on Plastic and Reconstructive Surgery will be held in Atlanta.

■ **organiser**
to organize / to stage

The convention was staged by the American Society of Plastic and Reconstructive Surgeons.

organisateur
organizer
A conference organizer, a meeting organizer.

comité organisateur
planning committee / organizing committee

■ **personnel (n)**
personnel / staff
During conventions, a numerous staff must be hired.

personnel de restauration / de secrétariat / de traduction
catering staff / secretarial staff / translating staff

programme
programme / program (US)
We've just received the programme of social events.

réservation
booking / reservation

effectuer une réservation
to book / to make a reservation
Book early to avoid disappointment!

■ **salle de conférence**
conference room
Our conference rooms have a seating capacity of about 100 each.

salle de réunion
function room / meeting room

■ **salon (foire, exposition)**
exhibition / fair / trade-fair
Los Angeles County Fair features acres of home arts, floral and agricultural displays, plus livestock judging and wine competition.

salon (hôtel, aéroport)
lounge
Weary businessmen can sit and relax in the hotel lounge.

■ **traitement de faveur**
red-carpet treatment
Business travellers expect red carpet treatment (ex: welcomme cocktail, complimentary drinks...).

■ **voyages de stimulation**
incentive travel (uncount) / incentive trips
Incentive travel is travel given by firms to employees, dealers or distributors as a reward for some special endeavour or as a spur to achievement.
Incentive trips originated in the USA during the 1960s.

1
LES CONFÉRENCES
Conferences

atelier
workshop

auditorium
auditorium
The main auditorium seats 350 people and features built-in audio visual equipment.

commission, jury
panel

groupe d'experts, de spécialistes
panel of experts

réunion - débat
panel discussion

conférence
conference

conférencier
lecturer / speaker

salle de conférences (amphithéâtre)
conference theatre / lecture theatre
This hotel features a spectacular conference theatre perfect for state-of-the-art audiovisual presentations.

donner une conférence
to deliver a conference / a lecture
He delivered a fascinating lecture on breast reconstruction.

assister à une conférence
to attend a conference
They attended a conference on macroeconomics.

conférence-vidéo
video-conference
Video-conferences can be a cheaper alternative to business trips since electronic sessions can accommodate as many participants as can fit in a studio.

congrès
congress / convention
Conventions can give a temporary boost to local employment.

congressiste
convention member / participant

palais des congrès
convention centre
This city boasts a multi-purpose convention centre with seating for over 600 delegates.

présider un congrès
to chair a convention

exposé
lecture / presentation

faire un exposé
to deliver a lecture / to make a presentation

He delivered a lecture on micro-surgery.

réunion
meeting
Meeting facilities.

être en réunion d'affaires
to be in a business meeting

réunion du Conseil d'Administration
Board Meeting
The Board Meeting will be held on Monday.

séminaire
seminar

symposium (pl.: symposia)
symposium
The symposium language will be English.

2 ÉQUIPEMENT POUR CONFÉFENCES Conference facilities

écouteur
earphone

écran
screen

écran de projection
projection screen

lutrin
lectern

machine à traitement de texte
word processor

magnétophone
tape-recorder

magnétoscope
video-cassette-recorder (VCR)

matériel audio-visuel
audio-visual equipment (AV)
In our purpose-built conference theatre a complete range of AV equipment is available for all functions.

ordinateur portable
laptop computer

photocopieuse
photocopier / photocopying machine

projecteur de diapositives
slide projector

projecteur de films
film projector / movie projector (US)

rétroprojecteur
overhead projector (OHP)

télécopieur
fax machine

service télécopie
fax service

TOURISME VERT
Green vacations

apiculture / apiculteur
beekeeping / beekeeper
Why not study the art of beekeeping this summer?

■ **arrière-pays**
hinterland (n)
They visited a tiny village somewhere in the hinterland of Portsmouth.

■ **ascencion en ballon**
ballooning
Ballooning is a gut-gripping experience.

    montgolfière
    hot-air balloon
    For a bird's-eye view of Napa Valley vineyards, ride in a hot-air balloon.

■ **autonome (hébergement, vacances)**
self-catering
Self-catering accommodation, self-catering holidays.
Small hotels have adapted their premises to provide self-catering units, meeting the need for flexibility in touring holidays.

■ **bicyclette**
bicycle / bike

    aller à bicyclette
    to bike / to cycle / to ride a bike / to wheel (US)
    They cycled the country roads of Provence last summer.
    Wheeling through Ireland is becoming a new fad.

    piste cyclable
    cycle path / cycle track (US)

In Yosemite national park, free shuttle buses and paved cycle paths link all of the valley's camping, lodging and visitor centers, making it possible to get along just fine without a car.

    promenade à bicyclette
    bike ride

    train + vélo
    "biking by train" (formule offerte par British Rail)

    vélo tout-terrain
    mountain bike

    cyclotourisme
    cycling holidays / cycle-touring
    A cycling holiday is both an invigorating and relaxed way to visit the Loire Valley.

calme (n)
peacefulness / stillness

    calme (adj.)
    peaceful / still

■ **campagne**
countryside

    auberge de campagne
    country inn

    route de campagne
    country road

■ **camper / faire du camping**
to camp / to go camping

    feu de camp
    camp-fire

    terrain de camping
    campground / campsite

Four hike-in campgrounds (charcoal braziers, pit toilets...) are open year-round by permit, available at the Bear Valley Visitor Centre.
Most of Death Valley campsites have scenic backdrops ranging from whispering sand dunes to sweeping mountain views.

■ canotage
boating
Boating holidays.

■ canyon
canyon
The canyon of the Main Salmon is the second deepest in North America, cutting through the Idaho Primitive Area.

■ chemin
lane (in country) / path (gén)

chemin de halage
tow-path
Tow-path cycling.

chemin de randonnée
country lane / footpath

■ circuit (aventure)
adventure holidays, adventure travel, adventure trips
Tired with your life of routine? Try adventure holidays!

circuit (découverte)
discovery trip

■ circuit
tour

colline
hill
Rolling hills, wooded hills...

■ croisière (fluviale)
canal cruise, river cruise / canal cruising, river cruising (activité)

The development of canal and river cruises has encouraged the establishment of small boat-hire companies and other services catering for the needs of the water-borne holidaymakers.

faire une croisière
to cruise / to go on a cruise

yacht de croisière
cabin-cruiser

découvrir une région, un pays au fil de l'eau
to cruise along canals, rivers.
Cruising along canals is one of the best ways to explore Holland.

■ descendre des rapides
to raft / to run rapids / to run a river

descente des rapides
rafting / rapids running / river running
This trip is one of the best water experiences: five days of action-packed rafting through unspoilt rainforest wilderness.
River running is becoming a popular warm weather attraction.

descente en eau vive
whitewater rafting
Try our whitewater rafting expedition that gets deep into the Australian wilderness.

■ descendre en rappel
to abseil

descente en rappel
abseiling
No previous abseiling experience is required for this expedition.

■ se détendre
to relax / to unwind
A boat trip on French canals is a good way to unwind.

■ écluse
lock

éclusier
lock-keeper

ouvir / fermer une écluse
to manœuvre a lock / to open / to
close the gates

■ **écologie**
ecology

écologiste
conservationist / ecologist / envi-
ronmentalist

écologique
ecological / environmental
*Removing rare plants, birds' eggs
affects the ecological balance.
Australian Environmental Policy:
"we endorse this philosophy -take
only pictures and leave only foot-
prints".*

les "Verts"
the Green Party / the Greenies
(fam)

■ **équitation**
horse-riding

monter à cheval
to ride a horse / to go horse-riding

promenade à cheval
horseback ride

piste cavalière
bridle path

■ **escalader**
to climb

varappe
rock-climbing
*You will find a variety of activities
available, from free nature walks and
art classes to raft rentals, horseback
rides and rock-climbing.*

varrapeur
rock-climber

■ **étoilé(e)**
starlit / starry
*You'll enjoy the crackle of a campfire
gazing at the starry night.*

dormir à la belle étoile
to sleep in the open

■ **évader (s')**
to escape (from) / to get away
from-it-all
*Concern about the environment has
spurred a growing number of Europeans
to seek alternatives to polluted beaches
and mobbed tourist capitals when they
get away from-it-all.*

besoin d'évasion
escapism

faune
fauna / wildlife

■ **ferme**
farm / farmhouse
*Gourmands who take time off in the win-
ter can arrange to spend a few days in a
farmhouse kitchen learning how to make
pâté de foie gras.*

vacances à la ferme
farm holidays
*Denmark has been particularly successful
in packaging farm holidays for the
international market.*

vivre à la ferme
to live on a farm

logis à la ferme
farm accommodation /
farm-based accommodation
*Farm accommodation is popular
among the growing number of holidaymakers whose life-style orienta-
tion is towards healthy food and
natural outdoor life.*

flore
flora

foule
crowd / mob (péjoratif) / throng
Situated snugly among the Leeward Islands in the West Indies, unaffected by throngs of noisy tourists, these islands offer visitors a mix of Old World charm and magnificent scenery.

bondé
crowded / packed / mobbed / thronged

surpeuplé
overcrowded

loin de la foule bruyante
"far from the madding crowd"

garde forestier
park ranger / ranger

■ **golf (sport)**
golf / golfing
Golf as a moderate form of exercice has soared in popularity among Europeans of all stripes.
Some EC countries are seeing a 100% increase in golfing each year.

terrain de golf
golf course / golf links
New golf courses are sprouting up everywhere in Europe.
Routenburn, Scotland, is an 18 hole par 68 golf course of 5,650 yards.

joueur de golf
golfer
More than a million golfers do 18 holes at least once a week in Britain and sportsmen on the Continent are fast discovering the game.

■ **grand air, plein air**
outdoors (n)
If your summer vacation itinerary includes experiencing the outdoors and seeing spectacular scenery, river rafting may be a mode of transportation you should consider.

jeux
games

jeux de plein air
outdoor games

■ **marcher**
to hike / to take a hike / to go for a walk / to take a walk / to walk

marche (activité)
hiking / walking

chaussures de marche
walking shoes, walking boots

■ **se mettre à (+ activité)**
to take to something / to take to do something
More and more tourists are taking to inland cruising.

■ **mode**
fashion / trend
While the trend towards green vacations has brought hard times to some conventional resort owners, it has been a godsend to country dwellers.

à la mode
fashionable / trendy

le tourisme vert est en vogue
Green vacations are catching on !

■ **nature**
nature
Across Europe, vacationers are rediscovering the joys of nature.

amoureux de la nature
nature-enthusiast / nature-lover

nature (sauvage)
wilderness
Popular parks from Acadia (Maine) to Yosemite (California) are jammed with visitors. The overcrowding is spreading raising environmental concern and threatening the wilderness "experience".

■ **parc national**
national park
Yosemite is America's first federal man-dated park and the model upon which the American national park system was based.

■ **paysage**
landscape / scenery
Rich in scenery and history, the Feather River region presents a varied topography-rocky canyons, fern-filled ravines, high mountains, leaf-covered foothills...

■ **pêcher**
to fish

pêcheur
angler (à la ligne) / fisherman
The icy, spring-fed waters of Hat Creek and Fall River present a challenge even to experienced anglers.

attirail de pêche
fishing tackle

canne à pêche
fishing-rod

■ **péniche**
barge
This newly-built hotel-barge explores the romantic region of the Yonne river.

naviguer en péniche
to barge / barging (n)
Barging is both educational and pleasurable.

■ **pittoresque**
picturesque / quaint / scenic
Collioure, the picturesque fishing port immortalized by Picasso, Matisse and Dufy is well worth a visit!

■ **protéger**
to protect

protéger les espèces en voie de disparition
to protect endangered / threatened species

■ **observer**
to watch

observation (activité)
watching

observation des baleines
whale-watching
This park's grandeur owes much to its varied seashore, popular for strolling, beachcombing and whale-watching.

observation des oiseaux
bird-watching
Point Reyes Bird Observatory is one of the best place for bird-watching.

■ **randonnée**
ramble / rambling (activité)
Rambling is the most popular activity in the Lake District.

faire de la randonnée
to go rambling / to ramble

randonneur
rambler / backpacker
Bear Valley is the gateway to more than 100 miles of trails, providing access to the park's remote beauty for ramblers or horseback riders.

chemin de randonnée
footpath / lane / trail

réserve
reserve / wildlife park

■ **route des vins / des fromages**
wine route / cheese route
Many British visitors follow the wine routes suggested in "Webster's Wine Tours of France".

faire la route des fromages
to go on a cheese taster's tour

faire la route des vins
to go on a wine taster's tour

■ **sentier**
footpath / trail

hors des sentiers battus
off the beaten track

spéléologie
potholing / spelunking (US)
Spelunking is exploring caves left in their natural state, wiggling along on hands and knees through narrow passages and tight spaces.

spéléologue
potholer / spelunker

■ **sport (s)**
sport (s)
Many tourists travel for sport. This may be participant sport, such as skiing or mountaineering, or spectator sport, such as attending the olympics or World Cup series.

faire du sport / pratiquer un sport
to do sport / to practise a sport

de sport (adj.)
sports (adj.)

équipements sportifs (infrastructure)
sporting facilities
The Inverclyde National Sports Training Centre possesses the best equipped and most comprehensive sporting facilities in Scotland.

■ **tranquille (allure, mouvement)**
leisurely (pace, movement)

Leisurely canal and river holiday cruising is particularly popular in the UK.

■ **trekking / faire du trekking**
trekking / to trek
They trekked for 2 months in Tibet.

randonnée à dos de chameau
Camel trekking

■ **tourisme fluvial**
inland waterway tourism
The British Waterways Board has encouraged the development of inland waterway tourism, and has helped to reopen disused canals to provide a network of interconnecting waterways throughout the country.

tourisme vert
"green" holiday / "green" vacations (US)
The emphasis is now on "green" holidays, where holiday-makers get in touch with nature.

■ **vacances actives**
action-packed holidays / activity holidays (ant.: passive vacationing)
There has been a move away from passive IT (Inclusive Tours) programmes for activity holidays.
The growth of activity holidays based around themes of sport, arts and crafts or hobbies can no longer be ignored by tour operators.

■ **vacances originales**
holidays with a difference / unusual holidays

VILLES
Towns and cities

abbatiale / abbaye
abbey
Glastonbury and its ruined abbey are steeped in legend.

■ **animé**
bustling / lively
Blackpool is a lively crowded, jostling resort, busiest during summer when the Lancashire mills close down for their annual holidays.

architecture
architecture
Southwark Cathedral is surrounded by warehouses, a produce market and some interesting new architecture.

   architecture baroque
   norman architecture

   architecte
   architect
   John Nash planned the rows of buildings that now form part of the outer circle of Regent's Park and line Park Square and Park Crescent.

■ **atout**
asset / draw / drawing card
Taiwan's biggest tourist draw is the National Palace Museum in Tapei which contains over 600 000 Chinese artifacts. Blackpool's promenade is its chief drawing card.

attrait
lure
Gujarat has many tempting lures: a festival of kites, a hilltop crowded with temples, sandy beaches...

autobus (urbain), autobus (inter-urbain)
bus / coach

   arrêt d'autobus
   bus stop

   arrêt facultatif
   request bus stop

berceau (civilisation)
cradle
The cathedral of Canterbury is the Mother Church of Anglican Christendom, the cradle of English Christianity.

bidonville
shanty town

bibliothèque
library
This library shelves some 1.5 million books.

boîte aux lettres
mail box (US) / letter box / pillar box

bureau de location (théâtre, spectacles)
box office / ticket booth / ticket office
Tickets are available for most London fringe theatres from the Fringe Box Office in St Martin's Lane.

cabine téléphonique
phone booth / pay station (US) / public phone

■ **capitale**
capital / capital city
Sacramento, California's capital, brims with pioneer history and gold-rush allure.

■ **cathédrale**
cathedral
Canterbury cathedral is a treasure house of architectural skills from Norman times onwards and contains a magnificent collection of stained glass.

   cloître
   cloister

   nef
   nave

   vitrail
   stained-glass window

centre commercial
shopping centre / shopping mall (US)

■ **centre ville**
inner city centre / city centre / downtown (US)
Unlike many big cities, San Francisco still has its government, financial and major retail centres located downtown. Walking is a good way to take a look at downtown San Diego's large entertainment complexes, small museums and shopping opportunities.

■ **dater (de)**
to date back (to) / to date (from)
Powis Castle -a red limestone castle near Welshpool dates from the late 13th century.

■ **déplacer (se) (dans une ville, un pays)**
to get around / to get round
London's Underground Railway or "Tube" is the easiest and quickest way of getting round London.

■ **droit d'entrée (exposition, musée, parc à thème ...)**
admission charge / entrance fee

One admission charge covers all activities.

   entrée gratuite
   admission free

église
church
Thatched cottages nestle in the shadow of the 15th century church, perched on a hill above the village.

époque
era
The Victorian era.

   d'époque
   period
   South of Regent's Park, many streets offer long vistas of period buildings. Harley St, Wimpole St and Wigmore St are three of interest.

espaces verts
green areas / open spaces

■ **exposition (art)**
exhibition
The Royal Academy stages its summer exhibition from May to August and mounts a number of other exhibitions throughout the year.

■ **festival**
festival
Over 180 artists from throughout the country display their works at Sausalito's annual Art Festival.
Cincinnati is a year-round haven for cultural events, festivals and music.

■ **flâner**
to stroll
They strolled by the river.
Experience Vizcaya -Miami's magnificent palace- and stroll through picturesque gardens enhanced by sculptured fountains and marble statuary !

■ **floralies**
flower show / horticultural exhibition

Holland's Floriade is the greatest flower show on earth!
Don't miss Floriade 1992, the World Horticultural Exhibition! It's a unique show of flowers, bulbs, plants, trees...

galerie (d'art)
art gallery
A unique collection of contemporary paintings, serigraphs and lithographs are for sale in this art gallery.

■ **galerie marchande**
shopping arcade

gratte-ciel
skyscraper

guide touristique
guide book / touring guide / tour book (US)

habitant
dweller / inhabitant
In Little Venice, London, the houses, pubs and restaurants reflect the literary and artistic tastes and occupations of the inhabitants.

hôtel de ville
city hall / town hall

■ **jardin public**
park / public gardens
It is the parks, more than any other feature, which make London unique among the world's great capitals.

■ **jardin botanique**
botanical gardens
Athens, north-east of Atlanta, is home to the State Botanical Gardens of Georgia. Set in a forest along a scenic river, the garden provides a perfect environment to collect, display and study the native plant life.

jardin tropical
tropical gardens

Miami's Parrot Jungle is a unique tropical gardens where exotic flowering trees and plants are complemented by the world's most beautiful birds.

■ **lèche-vitrine**
browsing / window-shopping

faire du lèche-vitrine
to browse / to window-shop
They window-shopped in Regent Street.

■ **lieux d'intérêt touristique**
places of interest / places to see
Cambridge's places of interest include the Colleges, the Folk Museum and Sedgwick Museum of Geology.

■ **(avoir) lieu**
to be held (at, in) / to take place (at, in)
Annual regattas are held at Burry Port in August.

■ **ligne (d'horizon, des toits...)**
skyline
The tallest structure on the San Francisco skyline is the Trans America Pyramid.
With a new skyline of thrilling colours and futuristic designs, Miami's downtown area has become an international business mecca.

maison à colombages
half-timbered house
Houses in Grope Lane are typical of the town's numerous half-timbered houses dating back to the Elizabethan era.

■ **marché**
market
When the produce markets left the area, Covent Garden's old buildings were saved and now form a thriving fashionable market for crafts, presents, souvenirs and clothes.

London's markets are as various as they are colourful and fascinating. Petticoat Lane Market -formerly a place where the local poor would buy old clothes and cast-offs of the rich- now attracts many tourists.

marché aux puces
flea market

■ métropole
metropolis
Atlanta is an exploding metropolis of some 2 million people.

monument
monument
Westminster Abbey displays over 1000 monuments and memorials to people notable in all aspects of British history.

monument classé
historic monument / listed monument

musée
museum

■ office de tourisme
Tourist Board / Tourism Office, Convention and Visitors Bureau
The London Tourist Board's main information centre is at Victoria Station. It will arrange hotel, theatre and tour bookings.

■ opéra (bâtiment)
opera house
Sydney's opera house is world-famous.

panorama, point de vue
vista
With the glinting gold Victoria Memorial at one end and the bulk of Admiralty Arch at the other, the Mall is in high summer one of the best vistas London can offer.

(se) perdre
to get lost / to lose one's way
They got lost in the maze of narrow streets.

■ piéton
pedestrian

passage pour piétons
pedestrian crossing / zebra crossing

pittoresque
picturesque / quaint
Woburn Walk is a quaint lane of bow-fronted well-preserved shops-everybody's idea of Dickens' London.

■ place
square
London's squares came into being in the 1630s, when Inigo Jones laid out Covent Garden.

■ plan de ville
city map

■ pont
bridge
Hamburg boasts 2,302 bridges-more than Venice and Amsterdam combined.

posséder (être fier de..., se vanter de...)
to boast
Bruges boasts picturesque canals.

■ poste
post office

poster (lettre)
to mail (a letter, a postcard...) / to post

■ quartier
area / district / neighborhood (US)

quartier commerçant
shopping district

quartiers pauvres
slums

quartier résidentiel
residential area / uptown (US)

remparts
ramparts / walls

■ **rue**
street
Cobbled streets (= pavées).

  rue principale
  high street / main street

  ruelle
  alley

salon des antiquaires
antiques fair

style gothique / moyenâgeux / roman / renaissance / contemporain
gothic / medieval / romanesque / renaissance / contemporary

  style gothique perpendiculaire anglais
  perpendicular style

■ **surpeuplé**
cramped / overcrowded

■ **syndicat d'initiative**
tourist information centre / visitor information center (US)

théatre
theatre / theater (US)
The RSC, the National Theatre and the summer open-air theatres in Holland Park and Regent's Park perform Shakespeare's work regularly.

  théatre en plein air / représentations en plein air
  open-air theatre / open-air performances

  pièce de théatre
  play

  comédie musicale
  musical
Don't miss "Me and My Girl" -a musical sparkling with energy and zany humour!

université
college / university
Trinity College, Dublin is well worth a visit!

■ **urbanisme**
town-planning

  urbaniste
  town-planner, urban planner

  équipement urbain
  town facilities

  réaménagement zones urbaines
  urban renewal

■ **ville**
city / town
Welcome to Miami, a vibrant metropolis fast becoming the city of the future!

  ville fantôme
  ghost town
Bodie is one of the best preserved mining ghost towns in America.

  ville natale
  birthplace
Stratford-upon-Avon was Shakespeare's birthplace.

■ **visite (d'une ville)**
sightseeing tour / tour
Tours start at 9am and leave every 30 minutes from convenient locations.

  visite guidée
  guided tour / escorted tour

  visite à pied
  walking tour
Enjoy a walking tour taking you back through Mercado's legendary past!

TRANSPORT
Transport, transportation (US)

— 1 —
TRANSPORT AÉRIEN
Air transport

aérodrome
airfield

■ **aérogare**
terminal

Stansted's terminal is being enlarged to cope with the overspill from Heathrow, Gatwick and Luton.

Don Muang Airport provides passengers with all the facilities you would expect at a modern international terminal.

■ **aéroport**
airport

Gatwick Airport is a mere 30 minutes from Victoria Station.

    taxe d'aéroport
    airport tax

■ **affréter (un avion)**
to charter (a plane)

They chartered a plane to Sydney.

■ **annuler (une réservation, un vol)**
to cancel

    annulation
    cancellation

■ **atterrir**
to land / to touch down

We have just landed at Gatwick Airport.

    atterrissage
    landing

    atterrissage forcé
    ditching / emergency landing / forced landing

    faire un atterrissage forcé
    to ditch

■ **avion**
aircraft (pl.: aircraft) / airplane / plane

    avion-cargo
    freighter

    avion charter
    charter plane

    avion gros porteur
    jumbo jet

    prendre l'avion
    to take the plane

    voyager en avion
    to fly / to travel by plane

    avion + croisière / avion + train / avion + voiture
    fly-cruise / fly-rail / fly-drive

■ **bagages**
baggage (US) / luggage (sg.: a piece of luggage)

    bagage à main
    carry-on luggage / hand luggage

    coffre à bagages
    overhead compartment / over-head bin (US)

May I ask you to stow your raincoat in the overhead compartment?

soute à bagages
baggage hold

franchise (bagages)
free baggage allowance

■ **(à) bord**
aboard / on board

bienvenue à bord
"welcome on board!"
Captain Smith and his crew are happy to welcome you aboard this boeing 767 to Atlanta.

en vol
in-flight (adj.)
In-flight entertainment, in-flight service...
Iberia is probably the only carrier in Europe to offer in-flight entertainment.

■ **billet d'avion**
air ticket / plane ticket

aller simple /aller retour
one-way ticket, single ticket /
return ticket / round-trip ticket (US)

boîte noire
black box / flight recorder

■ **boutique hors-taxe**
duty-free shops / tax-free airport shop
Duty-free shops are a handy place to spend a little time and money on a dull journey.
For the operators of tax-free airport shops, bored travellers mean booming turnovers.

achats hors-taxe / ventes hors-taxe
duty-free purchases / duty-free sales
The single market is soon to put an end to duty-free purchases within the
European Community; if duty-free sales disappear, air fares will increase sharply.

classe affaires
business class

classe économique
economy class
In general terms, on short flights there is not a lot of difference between economy and business classes. This contrasts with transatlantic and Far Eastern long-haul flights.

passager en classe économique
economy passenger

■ **compagnie aérienne**
airline
European airlines are beginning to introduce Frequent Flier Programs (FFPs), more specifically targeted toward business travellers than the general catch-all approach of those in North America.

■ **complet**
booked up / fully booked

■ **correspondance**
connection / connecting flight

correspondance entre deux lignes aériennes
interline connection

passagers en correspondance
connecting passengers

■ **décalage horaire**
jet-lag

souffrir du décalage horaire
to be jet-lagged

■ **décoller**
to take off
We shall take off shortly.

décollage
taking-off

■ **débarquer**
to deplane / to disembark / to get off the plane

carte de débarquement
landing card

déréglementation
deregulation
Deregulation may mean lower air fares, so more passengers and more over-crowding in the sky.

dérouter (un avion)
to divert / to re-route (a plane)

■ **desservir**
to link / to serve
We now serve nine major European cities.

■ **destination**
destination

départ à destination de...
departure to ...

■ **embarquer**
to board (a plane) / to embark / to get on (a plane)
Economy class passengers are requested to board now.

embarquement
boarding
Boarding will take place according to the seat numbers shown on the boarding cards.

carte d'embarquement
boarding card / boarding pass

porte d'embarquement
boarding gate
Immediate boarding! Passengers for this flight should proceed to Gate 8.

pré-embarquer
to pre-board
Such passengers as unaccompanied minors (UMs) are normally pre-boarded.

pré-embarquement
pre-boarding

■ **encombrement (aérien)**
air congestion / backup (US)
Big improvements will have to be made to ease air congestion over Britain.

le ciel est encombré
the skies are busy / the skies are crowded

■ **enregistrer (bagages)**
to check in
enregistrement

check-in
advanced check-in / separate check-in...

aire d'enregistrement des passagers
check-in area

comptoir d'enregistrement
check-in counter / check-in desk

équipage / personnel navigant
crew
The cabin crew have a number of duties to perform both before the passengers board and during boarding.

membres d'équipage
crewmembers

■ **escale**
layover (US) / stopover

faire escale (à)
to lay over (at) (US) / to stop over (at)
Passengers have to stop over at Atlanta and change plane to San Francisco.

espace aérien
air space
Europe has unnecessarily fragmented its air space.

fiabilité, sérieux
reliability
It's surely one of the best airlines in terms of reliability and service!

fiable
reliable

flotte aérienne
fleet

fuseau horaire
time-zone

horaire
schedule
This airline offers you convenient schedules and immediate connections spanning four continents!

hôtesse (de l'air)
air-hostess / cabin attendant (C.A.) / flight attendant
Cabin attendants must ensure that passengers fasten their seatbelts.

■ **liaison (aérienne)**
airlink / link
The decision made by TWA to discontinue several air links led to general protest.
The era of glasnost spurred both Pan Am and Aeroflot to search for a high-capacity airlink.

■ **lignes intérieures**
domestic airlines / feeder airlines

lignes régulières
scheduled airlines (ant.: non-scheduled airlines)
When charter flights developed, scheduled airlines introduced fare reductions, tourist, then economy class.

long courrier / moyen courrier
long haul / medium haul

navette
shuttle / shuttle bus
You will be transferred to your hotel in our complimentary shuttle.

ouvrir (une ligne)
to open (an air route, a regular flight...) / to begin (a new route, scheduled flights...)
Pan Am and Aeroflot are two of the world's pioneering airlines, with traditions of opening new air routes and flying long distances.

paralyser
to cripple
Air traffic was crippled by the Gulf War.

parcours
route
There are two Airbus routes running directly to all terminals at Heathrow, picking up at 13 points throughout the main hotel areas of Central London.
Charles Lindbergh surveyed transpacific and transatlantic routes for Pan Am.

partir
to depart / to leave
Today more than 600 Thai International flights depart Bangkok each week for 72 destinations in 36 countries across four continents.

pass aérien
air pass

■ **passager**
passenger
Since 1975, the number of air passengers in Europe has grown on average by nearly 6% a year far faster than governments or airlines predicted.

In the U.S.A., passenger numbers more than doubled in the decade after deregulation.

piste (d'envol, d'atterrissage)
airstrip / runway

ponctualité
ponctuality
Neither the staff nor passengers are happy with the airline's ponctuality record.

quasi-collision
near-miss
Air traffic has increased to the extent of causing air congestion especially during the peak season and grim stories of near-misses are reported.

règlementation / règlement
regulations / rules
As part of our flight is over the water, international regulations require that we demonstrate the use of life-jackets.
No regulations have been introduced to prevent airlines from slashing prices.

règlement de propriété des compagnies aériennes
airline-ownership rules

■ retarder (un vol)
to delay (a flight)

retardé (de...)
delayed (by...) (ant.: on time)
Almost a quarter of all intra-European flights were delayed by more than fifteen minutes last year.

rouler (avion)
to taxi
The aircraft leaves the ramp, taxies to the runway, lines up and takes off.

■ sécurité
safety / security
For your safety, please study the passenger safety information card when boarding the aircraft.

consignes de sécurité
safety instructions

sol (au)
ground (on the)
SAS excels on the ground where it has started city centre check-ins.

personnel au sol
ground staff
This airline boasts an efficient ground staff.

supprimer
to cancel (a flight) / to discontinue (an airlink)
This airline is going through dire financial straits; several airlinks will have to be discontinued.

sortie de secours
emergency exit

tarif
fare / rate

tarif excursion
APEX fare

titre de transport
ticket

■ trafic aérien
air-traffic
Investment in better air-traffic control equipment, together with a redesign of the routes used by aircrafts should free more airspace.

contrôleur aérien
air-traffic controler

transfert
transfer

■ transporter (passagers)
to carry (passengers)
The Jumbo Jet can carry up to 500 passengers.

transporteur aérien
carrier / air carrier
Foreign carriers should be allowed to compete for French domestic passengers to keep fares as low as possible.

turbulence
turbulence (uncount)
Turbulence caused the plane to turn over.

■ **vol**
flight

> **vol charter**
> charter flight
>
> **vol direct**
> non-stop flight
>
> **vol intérieur**
> domestic flight
>
> **vol régulier**
> scheduled flight, regular service
>
> **plan de vol**
> flight plan

zone fumeur / zone non-fumeur
smoking area / no-smoking area/ non-smoking area
The smoking area is located at the rear of the aircraft.

> **détecteur de fumée**
> smoke detector

2
TRANSPORT FERROVIAIRE
Rail transport

■ **billet**
ticket

> **billet demi-tarif**
> half-fare ticket

prix du billet
fare

contrevenant
fare-dodger
Fare-dodgers will be prosecuted.

distributeur automatique
ticket machine

buffet
refreshment room

bureau des objets trouvés
lost-property office / lost and found office (US)

■ **carte (de train) (abonnement général)**
railcard / pass / railway pass / railroad pass (US)

> **carte vermeil**
> senior citizen railcard
>
> **carte d'abonnement**
> season ticket / commuter pass / commuter ticket (US)
>
> **abonnement mensuel / trimestriel / annuel**
> one-month commuter pass, monthly ticket / three-month commuter pass / yearly ticket

chariot à bagages
luggage trolley

■ **chemins de fer**
railways / railroads (US)
During the 19th century, railroads spread across Europe and North America. They formed the first successful system of mass transportation.

> **chemins de fer britanniques / américains**
> British Rail / Amtrak

■ **circuler (train)**
to run
Trains to Gatwick Airport run every hour from Victoria Station.

■ **compartiment**
compartment
He only travels in first-class compart-ments.

compartiment fumeur / compartiment non-fumeur
smoking compartment / non-smoking compartment

■ **composter (un billet)**
to date-stamp (a ticket)
Don't forget to date-stamp your ticket before getting on the train.

machine à composter
date-stamping machine

■ **consigne (bagages)**
left-luggage office / baggage-room (US) / locker storage

consigne automatique
luggage-lockers

contrôleur
ticket-collector
The ticket-collector clips (= punches) the tickets.

■ **correspondance (train)**
connection / connecting train
Is there a connecting train to Glasgow?

dérailler
to leave the metals / to run off the rails

descendre (du train)
to get off (the train)
Don't forget to get off at the next station!

■ **desservir**
to call (at)
The 10 o'clock train calls at every station between Chatham and London.

■ **gare**
station / railway station
Brunel designed Paddington Station in the 19th century and the first regular omnibus service began.

gare routière
coach station / bus depot (US)

chef de gare
station master

aller chercher quelqu'un à la gare
to meet somebody at the station

mener quelqu'un à la gare
to see somebody to the station

guichet
ticket office
You can buy your ticket either at the ticket office or from a machine.
/

horaires
timetable / schedule (US)

indicateur
railway schedule / railroad schedule (US)

kiosque
bookstall / newsstand (US)

■ **lignes de banlieue**
commuter lines / suburban lines

grandes lignes
inter-city lines

lignes secondaires
branch lines
Branch lines are being restored and offer rides through picturesque scenery and a visit to the railway museum.

■ **métro**
undergroud / the Tube (London) / subway (US)
The Underground or Tube is the fastest and easiest way to get around Central London.

station de métro
underground station / tube station

■ **monter (dans un train)**
to board (a train) / to get on (a train) (ant.: to get off)

place (train)
seat

place côté fenêtre / place côté couloir
window seat / aisle seat

prendre le train (pour se rendre à son travail)
to commute
Many teachers commute on the high-speed train everyday.
Commuting to work can be a trial!

usager (régulier, banlieusard)
commuter

quai (train)
platform
On the platform an electronic board will remind you that the next train to Rochester is due at 11 a.m.

quitter la gare (train)
to depart from the station / to leave the station / to pull out of the station
I'm afraid you've missed the train to Brentwood! It has just pulled out of the station.

relier
to connect / to link

France's high-speed train network will be extended so as to link the Chunnel (Channel + Tunnel) with cities like Brussels.

relié (à)
connected (with) / linked (with)
All main line stations -that is the Intercity service to all parts of Britain- are connected with the Underground service.

relié par chemin de fer
linked by rail

réseau (ferroviaire)
(railway) network
In Europe, there is the Eurocity network linking about 200 towns and cities.

retardé
delayed / late
Is the train to Manchester delayed?

salle d'attente
waiting-room

supplément
excess fare

train
train
Most trains have air-conditioned coaches with wide, double-glazed windows, and reclining seats if you're travelling first class.

train auto-couchettes
motorail
Day or night motorail takes the stress out of long distance driving.

train à crémaillère
cog-wheel train

train direct
fast train / through train

T.G.V.
bullet train / high-speed train

funiculaire
cable-railway

omnibus
slow train

train+auto
rail-drive

train de marchandises
freight train

voyager en train
to ride a train / to travel by train
When you ride a train, you can relax and avoid the hassles of traffic.

voyage en train
train journey / train ride

wagon
carriage / car (US) / coach / railcar (US)
The Napa Valley Wine Train shuttles wine- lovers from vineyard to vineyard in vintage railcars.

wagon-lit
sleeping car / sleeper (US)

wagon restaurant
buffet car / dining car / restaurant car

wagon à deux étages (US)
double-decker car (US)

─── **3** ───

TRANSPORT MARITIME
Sea transport

accoster
to come alongside

■ **aéroglisseur**
hovercraft

■ **amarrer**
to tie up

The boat was tied up alongside a crumbling jetty.

■ **ancre**
anchor

être à l'ancre/ jeter l'ancre / lever l'ancre
to lie at anchor / to cast anchor, to drop anchor / to weigh anchor
They cast anchor in a secluded harbour.

ancrage
anchorage
At the southernmost tip of Key Biscayne, anchorage is limited to three nights per month per vessel.

appareiller (bateau)
to get under way

■ **bateau**
boat / ship (fem.)

bateau à aubes
paddle-boat / paddle-wheel boat
In Augusta, visitors can stroll along the banks of the Savannah River or enjoy a moonlit cruise aboard a replica 19th century paddle-boat.

bateau de croisière
cruise liner / cruise ship
Our cruise ships offer all the amenities of a resort hotel.

bateau à vapeur
steamboat

bateau mouche
pleasure steamer

■ **(à) bord**
aboard / on board / shipboard
Aboard, all your needs are covered in your overall cruise cost with the exception of incidental items such as wine, cigarettes, laundry, shore excursions...
We offer you the best-informed and most convenient way of seeing the Galapagos islands, combining on-board lectures

with in-situ excursions ashore to study the flora and the fauna.
The shipboard environment which we have created allows families to experience a bonding of sorts; they tell us that they leave the ship feeling closer as a family unit.

livre de bord
log-book

■ cabine
cabin

cabine intérieure / extérieure
inside cabin, cabin without a view / outside cabin, cabin with a view
The price per passenger ranges from £800 in a two-berth inside cabin to £1500 for a single-berth outside cabin.

cabine de luxe
stateroom
All our staterooms are handsomely appointed.

■ cap
cape
Magellan rounded Cape Horn and came north again up the coast of Chile.

mettre le cap (sur)
to head (for)

cargo
cargo-boat / freighter

compagnie de navigation
shipping company

■ couchette (bateau)
berth
Accommodation is in spacious two-berth cabins with all the comfort you may require.

■ croisière
cruise

Why not try expedition cruises to exotic lands?

croisière sur un lac / sur une rivière
lake-cruise / river-cruise

croisière à thème
special-purpose cruise
Special-purpose cruises are getting more and more popular with those interested in architecture, archeology, wild life...

faire une croisière / partir en croisière
to cruise / to go on a cruise / to take a cruise
Cruising is by far the best way to see Alaska, because so much of its beauty lies near the shoreline.

■ à destination (de) / en partance (pour)
bound (for)
Step aboard a Love Boat bound for Alaska and enter a world unlike anything you have ever experienced before.

ferry
ferry / ferry-boat
Ferries from Long Beach and San Pedro shuttle passengers to and from Avalon on an hourly basis.

■ embarquer
to board / to embark / to go on board

équipage
crew
Our yachts, taking a maximum of 12 persons are fully staffed with crew, steward and chef.

itinéraire
itinerary
This newly refurbished ship recently began an exclusive itinerary to the Abacos

Islands in the Northern Bahamas, featuring visits to four separarte islands.

■ loger
to accommodate
Increasing numbers of vacationers are opting for vessels accommodating fewer passengers and able to take them to quiet ports and secluded beaches.

maritime
seafaring
Great Britain has always been a seafaring nation.

■ naufrage
shipwreck
The crew perished in a shipwreck.

faire naufrage
to be shipwrecked
They were shipwrecked off the Bahamas.

navette
shuttle

effectuer la navette (bateau, véhicule...)
to shuttle

■ naviguer
to sail
For an unforgettable departure be on deck as you sail through San Francisco's legendary Golden Gate Bridge.

faire le tour du monde en bateau
to sail round the world

■ paquebot
liner
When you take a cruise on our luxury liner, you enter a world of pleasure and relaxation where comfort, wining and dining and entertainment are of the utmost importance.

passerelle (bateau)
gangway

■ phare
lighthouse
The lighthouse on South Stack, a rocky island off Holyhead Mountain, was built in 1809.

■ pont (bateau)
deck

sur le pont
on deck
Relax out on deck as your ship glides past forests in a thousand shades of green.

pont promenade
promenade deck / sun deck

jeux
deck-games / deck-sports
Deck-games range from volley-ball, and shuffleboard to skeet shooting and paddle tennis.
You will need clothes and footwear suitable for deck-sports.

■ port
harbour / port
The lack of a political consensus among the Twelve is preventing action for developing port infrastructures on the Atlantic and the Mediterranean seaboards.

port d'escale
port of call

port de plaisance
marina / yachting harbour

■ quai (bateau)
quay / wharf (pl.: wharves)

■ traversée (maritime)
crossing / sea-crossing / voyage

première traversée / traversée inaugurale
maiden voyage

Built in 1960 by Metro Goldwyn Mayer, the Bounty has sailed over 70000 miles including her maiden voyage to Tahiti for the filming of "Mutiny on the Bounty".

faire une bonne traversée / une mauvaise traversée
to have a smooth crossing / a rough crossing

sauver
to rescue

> **sauvetage**
> rescue

> **bouée de sauvetage / canot de sauvetage / gilet de sauvetage**
> life-buoy / life-boat / life-jacket, life-vest (US)

■ **(à) terre**
ashore / on-shore
Spend your time ashore discovering the special flavour of each port of call.
On-shore excursions are not included in the price we are quoting.

voies navigables
inland waterways
Holland is criss-crossed by a vast network of inland waterways.

TRANSPORT ROUTIER
Road transport

aire de repos
rest area

> **aire de stationnement**
> parking area

amende
fine / ticket (US)

■ **artère principale**
main thoroughfare

■ **assurance**
insurance

> **assurance au tiers**
> third party insurance

■ **auto-stoppeur**
hitch-hiker

> **faire de l'auto-stop**
> to hitch-hike
> *They intend to hitch-hike to Greece.*

avenue
avenue / parkway (US)

■ **banlieusard**
commuter
Reaching the Golden Gate Bridge is a bumper-to-bumper ordeal for commuters from Marin County.

> **se rendre au travail en voiture (trajet quotidien)**
> to commute

camping-car
motorhome / camper / recreational vehicle / van

caravane
caravan / trailer (US)

■ **carte grise**
car licence

> **carte routière**
> map / road-map
> *Free maps and guides for visitors can be obtained from the London Tourist Board.*

■ **ceinture de sécurité**
seat-belt

> **attacher (ceinture)**
> to fasten (seatbelt) / to buckle up (US)
> *"Buckle up! It's the law!"*

■ **circulation**
traffic
Suburban sprawl has meant clogged traffic over ever greater commuting distances as residents move farther and farther from the urban cores in search of affordable homes.

> **code de la route**
> highway code / road regulations (US)

> **déviation**
> detour (US) / diversion

> **essence**
> gas (US) / petrol

> > **station service**
> > filling station (US) / gas station (US) / petrol station

> > **le plein!**
> > full tank!

> > **faire le plein**
> > to fill (a car) up

■ **embouteillage**
bottleneck / congestion / tailback / traffic-jam
The new four-lane highway from Albertville should put an end to the appalling bottlenecks that have plagued the area.

> **embouteillé**
> clogged / congested / jammed

■ **emmener (quelqu'un en voiture)**
to give (someone) a lift
Can you give me a lift to London?

■ **heures de pointe**
peak hours / rush hours (ant.: slack hours)
Avoid taking the Tube at rush hours! All London stations are teeming with commuters.

impasse
blind-alley / cul-de-sac

■ **kilométrage illimité**
unlimited mileage

■ **limitation de vitesse**
speed limit
Do not exceed the speed limit! Highway speed limit is 55mph unless otherwise posted.

■ **louer (véhicule)**
to rent
Why not rent a convertible?

> **agence de location de voitures**
> car rental agency

> **conditions de location**
> rental terms

> **contrat de location**
> rental agreement

panneau (signalisation)
road sign

■ **parking**
car park / parking-lot (US)

> **parc de stationnement (plusieurs niveaux)**
> multi-storey car park

> **se garer**
> to park
> *Can I park my car somewhere round here?*
> *You can't park here, you're on a double yellow line!*

■ **péage**
toll

> **poste de péage**
> toll booth

> **route à péage**
> toll road / turnpike (US)

périphérique
by-pass / ring road / underpass

permis de conduire
driving licence / driver's licence (US)

plaque minéralogique
licence plate (US) / number plate / registration plate

réseau routier
road network

■ **route**
road

> **route nationale**
> highway (US) / A road (GB) / interstate (US)

> **autoroute**
> motorway (GB) / freeway (us-no toll) / turnpike (us-toll)

emprunter une route
to take a road
Take the first road on the left after the roundabout. Then it's straight on!

sortie d'autoroute
exit

■ **taxi**
cab / taxi / taxicab
They'll take a taxi back to the hotel.

> **héler un taxi**
> to wave down a taxi

> **station de taxis**
> taxi rank / taxi stand (US)
> · *There's a taxi rank just outside the airport.*

> **chauffeur de taxi**
> taxi driver

■ **transports en commun**
public transport

virage
bend / curve

> **virage en épingle à cheveux**
> hairpin bend

FORMALITES (ASSURANCE, CHANGE, DOUANE, SANTE)
Formalities (insurance, exchange, customs, health)

ambassade
embassy

animal (domestique)
pet
Pets brought into Germany must have current vaccination certificates.

■ **assurance**
insurance (uncount)
The holiday costs £589 plus insurance and airport taxes.

assurance annulation
cancellation insurance

assurance au tiers
third party insurance / Collision Damage Waiver (US) (= CDW)

assurance tous risques
comprehensive insurance / Full Collision Waiver (US) (= FCW)

assurance individuelle
Personal Accident Insurance (US) (=PAI)

s'assurer (contre)
to insure oneself (against)
You must think about insuring yourself against unexpected medical expenses or loss of baggage while abroad.

être bien assuré
to be properly insured
We strongly recommend that you and all members of your party be properly insured as soon as you book your holiday.

assuré (n)
insured party

contrat d'assurance
contract
Can a contract be tailor-made to our needs or are they standard in form?

assureur
insurer / insurance broker

carte de crédit
credit card
Major credit cards are generally accepted at British hotels, restaurants, shops and rental agencies.
Major credit cards are honored!

carte d'identité
identity card

■ **change**
exchange / foreign exchange

bureau de change
currency exchange bureau / currency exchange office

changer (de l'argent)
to exchange (a sum of money)

taux de change
exchange rate / rate of exchange
The exchange rate is the rate at which a sum of money is exchanged for an equivalent sum of money of another country's currency.

chèques de voyage
traveller's cheques / traveler's checks (US)

citoyen
citizen

citoyenneté
citizenship

■ **(se) conformer (à)**
to abide (by) / to comply (with)
Passengers must comply with airline regulations.

conformément aux règlements en vigueur
in accordance with the present regulations / in compliance with the regulations now in force

consulat
consulate

■ **couvrir**
to cover
Infants under two years of age are covered by their parents' insurance policy.

couverture
cover
You should carefully check the cover afforded by this policy.

portée de la couverture
extent of cover

■ **déclarer (douane)**
to declare

rien à declarer
nothing to declare / "green channel" (ant.: goods to declare / "red channel")

dégâts
damage

dégâts des eaux
flooding

■ **devise**
currency
Visitors may bring in Thailand any amount of foreign currency for personal use, but

that amount taken out should never exceed that declared upon entry.

devise faible /devise forte
soft currency /hard currency

■ **douane**
customs

passer la douane
to go through the customs
We went through the customs at Chicago O'Hare Airport.

droits de douane
customs duties

payer des droits de douane
to pay customs duty (on) / to pay duties (on)
Duties must be paid on automobiles, VCRs, cameras....

passible de droits de douane
dutiable

■ **(avoir) droit**
to be entitled (to)
You will be entitled to free prescriptions.

■ **entrer dans un pays**
to enter a country
A visa is requested to enter Burma and China.

■ **étranger (adj.)**
foreign

à l'étranger
abroad
Why not go abroad for the Easter holidays?

■ **exclure**
to exclude
Your holiday price excludes Collision Damage Waiver or Personal Accident Insurance.

exiger
to request / to require (usu. passive)
You are required to pay the balance shown on the invoice at least 8 weeks before departure.

■ **frontière**
border
She lives in the Pyrenees near the Spanish border.

passer la frontière
to cross the border
They crossed the border into Argentina.

gratuit
free / free of charge
Free insurance is provided for children travelling with their parents.

■ **immigration**
immigration
The government has just decided to put stricter controls on immigration.

service de l'immigration (aéroport, frontière, port...)
Immigration / Immigration Control
Your passport will be checked at the Immigration Control.

■ **inclure**
to include
This insurance includes cover under the 24-hour emergency service.

inclus
included

■ **indemnité**
compensation (uncount) / compensation payments
No compensation will be payable in such circumstances!

indemniser
to compensate (for)
We'll compensate you for a flight delay extending to 24 hours, because of adverse weather conditions, *mechanical breakdown, strike or industrial action.*

demande d'indemnisation
claim

■ **s'informer (de)**
to acquaint oneself (with)
You should acquaint yourself with up-to-date health and visa requirements for your journey prior to departure.

loi
law
"Respect for the law is the foundation of civilized living".

■ **maladie**
disease / illness

tomber malade
to be taken ill

■ **nationalité**
nationality
French nationality / British nationality...

double nationality
dual nationality

obligatoire
compulsory / mandatory / obligatory

panne
breakdown

tomber en panne
to breakdown

■ **passeport**
passport
Allow at least 6 weeks for obtaining a passport.

passeport en cours de validité
valid passport / fully valid passport
A valid passport is essential for travel to destinations in this brochure.

quarantaine
quarantine / quarantine period
All animals brought into the British Isles are subject to a six-month quarantine period.

réglementation
regulation(s)

■ **restriction**
restriction

    imposer des restrictions
    to impose restrictions (on)
    Some countries impose restrictions on visitors.

■ **santé**
health

    réglementation de la santé
    health regulations

■ **vaccination**
inoculation / vaccination

Vaccination against smallpox is compulsory.

    se faire vacciner (contre)
    to get vaccinated (against)
    You'd better get vaccinated against cholera, yellow fever and other tropical diseases if you intend to go to Africa.

en vigueur
in force

    entrer en vigueur
    to come into force
    The decree came into force last week.

■ **visa**
visa

    faire une demande de visa
    to apply for a visa

    obtenir un visa
    to get a visa, to obtain a visa
    Your travel agent will be happy to assist you to obtain visas.

accompagnateur
courier / tour escort / tour leader
Couriers are employed by coach companies or tour operators to supervise and shepherd groups of tourists participating in tours.

affluence (touristique)
influx
The influx of tourists has dropped lately.

■ agence de voyages
travel agency
A license is required to set up a travel agency.

agent de voyages
travel agent
Travel agents earn their revenue in the form of commission on sales.

agent de comptoir
counter clerk

allouer
to allocate
The client is allocated a booking reference number.

attirant
alluring / attractive

attirer
to attract / to lure
The Barcelona Olympics, Seville'Expo'92, the Floriade Show in The Hague, the Colombo'92 celebrations in Genoa, are attracting holiday-makers back to Europe in 1992.

■ autorisation / permis
licence / license (US)
A license is requested to set up business.

auxiliaire (service) (adj.)
ancillary
Ancillary tourism services.

bénéfice
profit

réaliser des bénéfices
to make a profit / to turn a profit

marge bénéficiaire
profit margin
Because profit margins on long-haul travel are higher, tour operators and travel agencies have happily encouraged the long-haul trend.

besoin
need

répondre aux besoins
to meet the needs
The Managing Director spoke about the airline's efforts to meet the needs of business and pleasure travellers.

■ billeterie
ticketing

billet
ticket
These tickets are neither transferable nor refundable.

émettre un billet
to issue a ticket

bouder (une destination)
to shun (a country, a destination)
Countries like Cyprus and Greece were shunned by tourists during the Gulf War.

■ brochure
brochure / leaflet

Brochure descriptions are based on the information obtained during visits made by our staff.
A leaflet with prices and detailed itinerary is available upon request.

■ chiffre d'affaires
turnover

The annual turnover in sales of souvenirs tops £5 m.
Last summer's turnover exceeded $3 million.

cible
target

Target audience / target market.

circuit de distribution
chain of distribution

The term "chain of distribution" is used to describe the methods by which a product or service is distributed from its manufacturing source to its eventual consumers.

commission
commission (uncount /count)

Each booking made through the travel agent brings a commission.
You will get commission on top of your salary.

comptabilité
accountancy / book-keeping

service comptable
accounts department

Please contact our accounts department for any further information you may require.

■ concurrence
competition

concurrence acharnée
cut-throat competition

concurrence loyale / déloyale
fair / unfair competition

être en concurrence
to compete (with)

The new regulations might enable American airlines to compete with European airlines.

■ conseil
advice (uncount)

conseiller / donner des conseils
to advise (so to do sthg) / to give advice

Travel agents advise prospective clients on resorts and facilities.

consommation
consumption

consommateur
consumer

Tours operators are selling dreams and their brochures must allow consumers to fantasise about their holiday, but it is also vitally important that consumers are not misled.

société de consommation
consumer society

crise
crisis / slump

The continent suffered its worst tourist slump in 1991.

critères
standards

satisfaire aux critères
to meet with standards

■ croissance
growth

Tourism is a key point of growth in the economy.

croître (augmenter) (de)
to grow (by) / to increase (by) / to rise (by)

Jobs in tourism will grow by 20% in the future.

dégrader
to damage / to spoil
The environment has been irretrievably damaged.

■ **demande**
demand
Hoteliers find it hard to cope with tourist demand at peak season.

la loi de l'offre et de la demande
the law of supply and demand

dépasser / excéder
to exceed / to top
Boosted by a series of world-class sporting, cultural and historical events, the tourist industry -Europe's biggest employer- is expecting the number of visitors to equal or exceed numbers in 1990.

dépenses
expenditure / spending
Visa International commissioned a research on holiday travel expenditure in Europe last year. The report revealed that Germany had the largest holiday bill.

dépliant
folder
Could you include folders about itineraries and prices?

diminuer
to decline / to decrease / to diminish
Air fares to the USA have decreased by 20%.

diminuer (petit à petit)
to taper off
Tourism in the Alps usually tapers off after the Easter holidays and ski resorts are quiet again.

documentaire (de voyage)
travelogue

■ **documentation touristique**
travel data / travel literature
Would you have special literature about adventure travel?

■ **économie (d'une région ,d'un pays ...)**
economy
Portugal's economy is still largely based on tourism.
Tourism is vital for Spain's economy since it accounts for 8% of GDP.

économique
economic
Economic crisis / economic issues / economic policy...

économies
savings

economiser
to save
Tour operators are trying to save money by buying in bulk.

économique
economical (= cheap)
VFR (Visiting Friends and Relatives) remains an economical way to spend vacations.

■ **échelonner (paiements, vacances...)**
to stagger (payment, holidays...)
The summer holidays are staggered in order to keep businesses running.

échelonnement / étalement
staggering

vacances échelonnées
staggered holidays

élastique (adj.) (demande, offre, prix)
elastic (ant.: inelastic)
Holiday travel is highly price elastic: lower prices will encourage an increase in the number of holidaymakers; business travel, however, is relatively price inelastic.

élasticité de la demande par rapport au prix
price elasticity of demand

élasticité du marché
market resilience

■ **enjeu**
stake
The stakes of this advertising campaign are pretty high.

être en jeu
to be at stake
Coastal development is at stake!

■ **étude de faisabilité**
feasability study

étude de marché
market research

exercice (comptabilité)
financial year

facture
bill / invoice
Your invoice will be sent within a week.

■ **familiariser**
to acquaint (with)
Seminars are organized to acquaint travel agents with new programmes and selling techniques.

■ **financer**
to finance / to fund
The new convention centre is being funded both by Local Authorities and private industry.

financement
financing / funding

■ **florissant**
booming / flourishing / thriving
Tourism in Ireland is booming / The Irish tourist industry is thriving.

flux (touristique)
flow
The flow of American visitors has increased steadily.

formation
training

stage de formation (en agence)
in-training programme
Most travel agencies offer in-training programmes.

fréquentation (touristique)
tourist attendance
As prosperity has put exotic travel destinations within the reach of many Europeans, ski resorts have suffered declines in attendance.

■ **gamme / éventail**
array (of) / range (of)
This resort offers a wide range of activities to suit all tastes.

bas de gamme / haut de gamme
down-market / up-market
The European tourist industry is advised to move upmarket and offer high quality services.

■ **industrie**
industry (uncount)
Tourism is now a major industry which accounts for over 5% of the world trade.

intermédiaire (n)
middleman

par l'intermédiaire de
through
It's best to book through a travel agent.

■ **investissement**
investment
There has been massive foreign investment in the tourist industry.

investir
to invest
The Turkish government has invested $220 million to build a new chain of sewage-treatment plants.

investisseur
investor
Investors are supporting the development project of the site.

jumelage (ville)
town twinning
A fantastic boom has been given to international tourism by the town twinning movement.

■ lancer un nouveau produit
to launch a new product
Underpricing a holiday is probably a good means to launch it.

frais de lancement
set-up costs

■ loisirs
leisure (uncount)
Leisure is an area of free choice and discretionary spending strongly influenced by national differences in climate, geography, culture and heritage.

société de loisirs
leisure society

■ marché
market
In the U.K., golf equipment is the largest sports equipment market with annual turnover of £175 million.
It is essential to define the market you're aiming at for each product.

part (de marché)
share
This tour operator commands a 30% share of the market for inclusive holidays.

pénétrer un marché
to break into a market

A foreign company would find it hard to break into the U.K. market, since most of its big travel companies combine tour operator and travel agency functions.

mercatique
marketing

agence de commercialisation
marketing board / marketing bureau
To produce a coordinated strategy for the promotion of tourism, several cities have opted for the formation of a marketing board made up of representatives from both the public and the private sectors.

stratégie de marketing
marketing strategy
Their marketing strategy development was very efficient.

métiers du tourisme
careers in tourism

■ niveau de vie
standard of living
The standard of living is usually held to be determined by the quantities of goods and services (including leisure) consumed.

objectif (n)
aim / goal / objective
Our objective is to provide a very upmarket, quality airline which offers unique and distinctive service.

option
option

prendre une option
to make a provisional reservation / to take out an option

ordinateur
computer
Availability is checked on the computer.

entrer des données dans l'ordinateur
to key data into the computer

parc à thème
theme park
Theme parks such as Eurodisney or Thorpe Park provide scope for a full day's entertainment.

■ **politique touristique**
tourist policy
For the most part, tourist policy is defined and implemented through national tourist boards.

définir une politique
to define a policy / to lay down a policy

■ **pouvoir d'achat**
purchasing power /
spending capacity (US)

prestataire de service
service provider / service supplier

prestation
service
Tourism demand is met by the concentrated effort of a wide range of tourist services.

prêt (n) (somme prêtée)
loan
The International Development Association (IDA) offers interest-free or low rate loans.

solliciter un prêt
to apply for a loan

accorder un prêt
to grant a loan
Governments aid the private sector by granting loans at preferential rates of interest for development schemes which are in keeping with government policy.

■ **prévoir**
to forecast / to foresee / to predict
Footwear specialists have detected the early signs of a boom in recreational walking, and foresee an increasing demand for walking and hiking shoes.

■ **prix / tarifs**
fares / prices / rates

prix attrayants
compelling prices

prix réduits
cut rates / discount fares / reduced prices / slashed prices

rapport qualité-prix
value for money
This tour will give you unrivalled value for money.

casser les prix
to slash prices /
to undercut prices

■ **produit**
product
New products such as artificial ski slopes and indoor tropical swimming paradises have become increasingly popular.

produit intérieur brut (PIB)
gross domestic product (GDP)
The tourist industry employs 6% of the workforce and accounts for 5.5% of the EC's GDP.

produit national brut (PNB)
gross national product (GNP)

professionnel (adj.)
professional
Since tourism is one of the world's largest industry, the role of the travel agent has become more and more professional.

■ profiter (de) / exploiter
to capitalize (on) / to cash in (on)

Tour operators did their best to capitalize on new tourist trends.

■ promouvoir
to foster / to promote

The Tourist Boards' main objective is to foster tourism within a country.
The European Commission has earmarked Ecu 750,000 to promote Europe as a tourist destination.

promotion touristique
tourist promotion

promotionnel / publicitaire
promotional

The promotional efforts of both government and private sector have greatly helped to attract more tourists.
Our promotional budget has increased by 10%.

tarif promotionnel
incentive fare

■ publicité (gén.)
advertising

The functional responsibilities of a national tourist board include advertising, sales promotion and public relations activities directed at home and overseas markets.

publicité (une)
ad / advert / advertisement

Here's an eye-catching advertisement to promote holidays in France.

campagne publicitaire / campagne publicitaire intensive
advertising campaign / advertising blitz

faire de la publicité
to advertise

Governments should advertise less popular attractions and regions while promoting the off-season.

■ recettes
receipts

Receipts from tourism grew by some 37% last year.

■ recherche
research (uncount)

faire de la recherche
to do research

Tourist Boards do research in order to get in-depth knowledge of holiday tastes.

■ relié (à)
connected (with) / linked (to, with)

Most agencies are linked to terminals which provide information on departures, seat availability from the computers of major airlines.

■ rembourser
to refund

Lost tickets are neither refunded nor replaced.

remboursement
refund

There are limited refunds on cancellation on most economy tickets.

non remboursable
non-refundable (ant.: refundable)

■ rentable
profitable

According to a 1990 survey, French hotels were the most profitable in Europe before tax.

rentabililté
profitability

In 1990, hotels in Austria, probably reflecting their proximity to eastern Europe, experienced a significant increase in profitability-per-room.

seuil de rentabilité
break-even point

They failed to reach the break-even point.

rentrer dans ses frais
to break even
Hoteliers broke even despite the perceptible drop in the influx of tourists.

représenter
to account (for)
Cyprus was badly hit by the Gulf Crisis as tourism accounts for 22% of its Gross Domestic Product.

répondre aux exigences
to meet demands
Tour operators always do their utmost to meet customers' demands.

réputation
reputation
Our reputation is based on providing quality holiday and good service.

réservation
booking / reservation
Sophisticated reservation systems involve the use of computers.

service de réservation
booking service / reservation service
The UK tourist offices provide a booking service called "Book A Bed Ahead" (BABA) for hotels and farmhouse accommodation through their Tourist Information Centres.

■ **revenu**
income / revenue
Tourism is the third most important source of revenue in the Falklands, after the traditional staples, fishing and wool.

revenu disponible
disposable income
The disposable income is the total income of households less income tax and national insurance contributions.

tranche des revenus élevés
high-bracket income (ant.: low-bracket income)

■ **saison**
season

haute saison / basse saison
high season, peak season / low season, off-peak season

saisonnier
seasonal
Hotels and restaurants hire a lot of seasonal workers.

solde (comptabilité)
balance

■ **subventions**
subsidies

subventionner
to subsidize

accorder des subventions
to grant subsidies
During the Gulf War, governments granted travel companies subsidies to tide them over the bad period.

sur-mesure, à la carte
tailor-made
Tailor-made packages, tailor-made tours.

■ **taxe**
tax

T.V.A.
V.A.T. (Value Added Tax)
The V.A.T. (Tour Operators) Order 1987 came into force in 1988 and imposes taxation on profit margins for any tours between EC countries.

T.V.A. comprise
V.A.T. included / including V.A.T. / inclusive of V.A.T.

■ **tourisme de loisirs**
recreational tourism (ant.: business tourism)

tourisme de masse
mass tourism
As Europe enjoys -and endures- another season of mass tourism, hospitality is fast becoming an exercise in damage control.

tourisme social
social tourism
The International Bureau of Social Tourism (BITS) has been active since 1963 as a base for the study of social tourism.

touristique
tourist
Spain re-evaluated its tourist policy in the late 1980s when it became locked into price wars for lower-spending mass tourists.

touristique (péjoratif)
touristy

touriste
tourist / visitor

faire du tourisme
To go sightseeing / to go on a sightseeing tour / to tour (a region, a country).

■ **vacances**
holidays / vacations (US)
Not all of us want to spend our holidays lying on a beach; some of us want vacations that turn our mind on, not off.

être en vacances
to be on holiday / to be on vacation (US) / to holiday / to vacation (US)
The Spanish spend more money on holidays than any other Europeans, yet they are the least adventurous, preferring to holiday at home.

vacances chez des amis / dans

la famille
VFR (Visiting Friends and Relatives) / VFR travel
The VFR market is a substantial and growing one in tourism.

vacancier
holiday-maker / vacationer (US)
Mediterranean resorts now have to compete for European holiday-makers with Florida and Barbados.

vivre du tourisme
to live off tourism
With 2 million people living off tourism, it is easy to understand why the government is urgently trying to head off the disaster.

■ **voyage**
journey / trip / voyage (= journey by boat only)
They went on a trip to the unspoiled islands of St. Kitts and Nevis.
There is a set of beautiful twin sisters in the Caribbean, which Christopher Colombus stumbled upon in 1493 during his voyage to the New World.

voyage organisé, "forfait"
I.T. (Inclusive Tour) / G.I.T. (Group Inclusive Tour) / package tour (ant.: independent tour)
A package tour is an arrangement by which transport and accommodation is purchased by the tourist at an all-inclusive price.

mini-séjour
short break
The short break market is booming!

voyager
to make a trip / to travel
They travelled round the world.

LISTE DES PRINCIPAUX PAYS ET DE LEURS HABITANTS

■ **Afghanistan**
Afghanistan

Afghan
Afghan

■ **Afrique du Sud**
South Africa

Sud-Africain
South African

■ **Algérie**
Algeria

Algérien
Algerian

■ **Allemagne**
Germany

Allemand
German

■ **Arabie Saoudite**
Saudi Arabia

Saoudien
Saudi Arabian

■ **Argentine**
Argentina

Argentin
Argentinian

■ **Australie**
Australia

Australien
Australian

■ **Belgique**
Belgium

Belge
Belgian

■ **Birmanie**
Burma

Birman
Burmese

■ **Bolivie**
Bolivia

Bolivien
Bolivian

■ **Brésil**
Brazil

Brésilien
Brazilian

■ **Bulgarie**
Bulgaria

Bulgare
Bulgarian

■ **Cameroun**
Cameroon

Camerounais
Cameroonian

■ **Canada**
Canada

Canadien
Canadian

■ **C.E.I. (Communauté d'Etats Indépendants) (ex U.R.S.S.)**
C.I.S. (Commonwealth of Independent States) (ex USSR)

■ **Chili**
Chile

Chilien
Chilean

■ **Chine**
China

Chinois
Chinese

■ **Chypre**
Cyprus

Chypriote
Cypriot (n), Cyprian (adj)

■ **Corée**
Korea

Coréen
Korean

■ **Cuba**
Cuba

Cubain
Cuban

■ **Danemark**
Denmark

Danois
Dane (n), Danish (adj)

■ **Egypte**
Egypt

Egyptien
Egyptian

■ **Equateur**
Ecuador

Equatorien
Ecuadorian

■ **Espagne**
Spain

Espagnol
Spaniard (n), Spanish (adj)

■ **Etats-Unis**
U.S.A. (United States of America)

Américain
American

■ **Ethiopie**
Ethiopia

Ethiopien
Ethiopian

■ **Finlande**
Finland

Finlandais
Finn (n), Finnish (adj)

■ **France**
France

Français
Frenchman (n), French (adj)

■ **Grande-Bretagne**
Great Britain

Britannique
Briton (n), British (adj)

■ **Grèce**
Greece

Grec, Grèque
Greek

■ **Guatemala**
Guatemala

Guatémaltèque
Guatemalan

■ **Guinée**
Guinea

Guinéen
Guinean

■ **Guyane**
Guyana

Guyanais
Guyanese

■ **Hollande**
Holland

Hollandais
Dutchman (n), Dutch (adj)

Pays-Bas
The Netherlands

■ **Hongrie**
Hungary

Hongrois
Hungarian

■ **Inde**
India

Indien
Indian

■ **Indonésie**
Indonesia

Indonésien
Indonesian

■ **Irak**
Iraq

Irakien
Iraqi

■ **Iran**
Iran

Iranien
Iranian

■ **Irlande**
Ireland

Irlandais
Irishman (n), Irish (adj)

■ **Islande**
Iceland

Islandais
Icelander (n), Icelandic (adj)

■ **Israël**
Israel

Israëlien
Israeli

■ **Italie**
Italy

Italien
Italian

■ **Jamaïque**
Jamaica

Jamaïcain
Jamaican

■ **Japon**
Japan

Japonais
Japanese

■ **Jordanie**
Jordan

Jordanien
Jordanian

■ **Kenya**
Kenya

Kénien
Kenyan

■ **Koweit**
Kuwait

Koweitien
Kuwaiti

■ **Liban**
Lebanon

Libanais
Lebanese

■ **Luxembourg**
Luxemburg

Luxembourgeois
Luxemburger (n), Luxemburg (adj)

■ **Lybie**
Lybia

Lybien
Lybian

■ **Malaisie**
Malaysia

Malais
Malaysian

■ **Malte**
Malta

Maltais
Maltese

■ **Maroc**
Morocco

Marocain
Moroccan

■ **Maurice**
Mauritius

Mauricien
Mauritian

■ **Mexique**
Mexico

Mexicain
Mexican

■ **Népal**
Nepal

Népalais
Nepalese

■ **Norvège**
Norway

Norvégien
Norwegian

■ **Nouvelle-Zélande**
New Zealand

Néo-zélandais
New Zealander

■ **Pakistan**
Pakistan

Pakistanais
Pakistani

■ **(Les) Philippines**
(The) Philippines

Philippin
Filipino (n), Philippine (adj)

■ **Pérou**
Peru

Péruvien
Peruvian

■ **Pologne**
Poland

Polonais
Pole (n), Polish (adj)

■ **Portugal**
Portugal

Portugais
Portuguese

■ **Roumanie**
Romania, Rumania

Roumain
Romanian

■ **Sénégal**
Senegal

Sénégalais
Senegalese

■ **(Les) Seychelles**
(The) Seychelles

Seychellois
Seychellois

■ **Singapour**
Singapore

Singapourien
Singaporean

■ **Somalie**
Somalia

Somalien
Somali (n), Somalian (adj)

■ **Soudan**
(The) Sudan

Soudanais
Sudanese

■ **Sri Lanka (ex-Ceylan)**
Sri Lanka (ex-Ceylon)

Ceylanais
Ceylonese

■ **Suède**
Sweden

Suédois
Swede (n), Swedish (adj)

■ **Suisse**
Switzerland

Suisse
Swiss

■ **Syrie**
Syria

Syrien
Syrian

■ **Thaïlande**
Thailand

Thaïlandais
Thai

■ **Tibet**
Tibet

Tibétain
Tibetan

■ **Tunisie**
Tunisia

Tunisien
Tunisian

■ **Turquie**
Turkey

Turc (n), Turque (adj)
Turk (n), Turkish (adj)

■ **Uruguay**
Uruguay

Uruguayen
Uruguayan

■ **Vénézuela**
Venezuela

Vénézuelien
Venezuelan

■ **Vietnam**
Vietnam

Vietnamien
Vietnamese

■ **Yougoslavie**
Yugoslavia

Yougoslave
Yugoslav (n), Yugoslavian (adj)

■ **Zaïre**
Zaire

Zaïrois
Zairean

SIGNES PUBLICS
Public signs

aire de pique-nique
picnic area

boutique
gift shop

casiers à bagages
baggage lockers

change
currency exchange

chemin de grande randonnée
hiking trail

défense d'entrer
no entry

défense de fumer
no smoking

défense de stationner
no parking

douane
customs

eau potable
drinking water

enregistrement des bagages
baggage check-in

feux autorisés
campfires

location de voiture
car rental

objets trouvés
lost and found

point de vue
viewing area

poste de secours
first aid

pouponnière
nursery

renseignements hôteliers
hotel information

retrait des bagages
baggage claim / luggage claim

toilettes
toilets, restrooms (US)

zone de jeux
playground

CORRESPONDANCE
Letter-writing

=== 1 ===
FORMULES D'INTRODUCTION
opening salutations

Madame, Monsieur
Dear Sir / Madam

Cher Monsieur / Chère Madame
Dear Sir / Dear Madam

Cher Monsieur X / Chère Madame X
Dear Mr X / Dear Mrs X

Messieurs (lettre adressée à une entreprise)
Dear Sirs (GB) / Gentlemen (US) (to address a company)

=== 2 ===
FORMULES DE POLITESSE
closing salutations

veuillez agréer l'expression de mes salutations distinguées
Yous Faithfully (formal) / Yours Sincerely (less formal) / Yours Truly (less formal)

cordialement
best wishes

=== 3 ===
LISTE D'EXPRESSIONS STÉRÉOTYPÉES
model sentences

dans l'attente d'une réponse / de vous lire
we are looking forward to hearing from you

j'accuse réception de...
I acknowledge receipt of... / Thank you for your letter of... / I'm pleased to acknowledge receipt of...

j'ai le plaisir de vous annoncer que...
I'm pleased to inform you that... / I'm pleased to let you know that...

j'ai le regret de vous informer que...
I'm sorry to inform you that... / I regret to inform you that...

je vous serais reconnaissant de bien vouloir confirmer votre réservation dans les meilleurs délais
I would be grateful if you would kindly confirm your reservation as soon as possible / in the nearest future

n'hésitez pas à nous contacter pour de plus amples détails
Should you require any further information, do not hesitate to contact us

une réponse rapide nous obligerait
an early reply would be appreciated

sauf réponse de votre part
unless we hear from you to the contrary

suite à votre lettre du...
following your letter of... / further to your letter of...

sous pli séparé
under separate cover

sous huitaine
within a week

nous nous tenons à votre entière disposition pour tout renseignement complémentaire
we remain at your entire disposal for any further information you may require

veuillez avoir l'obligeance de nous répondre par retour du courrier
would you be so kind as to reply by return of post

veuillez confirmer par écrit
kindly confirm in writing / please confirm in writing

veuillez excuser notre retard
please accept our apologies for the delay / we apologize for the delay

veuillez nous faire savoir dès que possible si ces conditions vous conviennent
will you let us know at your earliest convenience whether these terms are acceptable / would you be so kind as to let us know if these terms are acceptable

veuillez trouver ci-joint la documentation touristique actuellement disponible
please find enclosed the travel literature presently available

votre lettre en date du...
your letter of...

votre lettre du 21 courant
your letter of 21st instant

votre lettre sous rubrique
your above-mentionned letter

votre telex du 9 écoulé
your telex of 9th ultimo

LEXIQUE FRANÇAIS

A

abbatiale 45
abbey

abbaye 45
abbey

abriter (de) 23
shelter (to) (from)

accompagnateur 68
courier, tour escort, tour leader

accoster 58
come alongside (to)

addition 31
bill, check (US), tab (US)

aérodrome 50
airfield

aérogare 50
terminal

aéroglisseur 58
hovercraft

aéroport 50
airport

affaires 35
business

affection 28
affliction, ailment, trouble

affluence (touristique) 68
influx

affréter (un avion) 50
charter (to) (a plane)

Afghan 77
Afghan

Afghanistan 77
Afghanistan

Afrique du Sud 77
South Africa

agence de voyages 68
travel agency

aire de pique-nique 83
picnic area

aire de repos 61
rest area

Algérie 77
Algeria

Algérien 77
Algerian

algues 23
seaweed

Allemagne 77
Germany

Allemand 77
German

allouer 68
allocate (to)

alpinisme 7
mountaineering, mountain-climbing

altipiste / altiport 7
snow runway, mountain landing strip

altitude 7
elevation

amarrer 58
tie up (to)

ambassade 64
embassy

aménagement du littoral 23
coastal development, shore development

aménagements pour les handicapés 18
facilities for the disabled, facilities for the handicapped, wheel-chair access

amende 61
fine, ticket (US)

Américain 78
American

amuse-gueule 31
appetizer

ancre 58
anchor

animal (domestique) 64
pet

animé 45
bustling, lively

annulation 18
cancellation

annuler 18
cancel (to)

annuler (une réservation, un vol) 50
cancel (to)

anse 23
cove

apiculteur 39
beekeeper

apiculture 39
beekeeping

appareiller (bateau) 58
get under way (to)

appartement 19
flat, apartment (US)

après-ski 7
after-ski

Arabie Saoudite 77
Saudi Arabia

archipel 23
archipelago

architecture 45
architecture

Argentin 77
Argentinian

Argentine 77
Argentina

arrhes 18
deposit

arrière-pays 39
hinterland (nom)

artère principale 61
main thoroughfare

ascencion en ballon 39
ballooning

ascenseur 18
elevator (US), lift

assurance 61, 64
insurance

atelier 37
workshop

atoll 23
atoll

atout 45
asset, draw, drawing card

atterrir 50
land (to), touch down (to)

attirant 68
alluring, attractive

attrait 45
lure

aube 12
dawn

auberge 20, 31
inn
auberge 31
country inn
auberge de jeunesse 20
hostel, youth hostel
community hotel (cotel, US)
auditorium 37
auditorium
Australie 77
Australia
Australien 77
Australian
auto-stoppeur 61
hitch-hiker
autobus (inter-urbain) 45
coach
autobus (urbain) 45
bus
autonome (hébergement, vacances) 39
self-catering
autorisation / permis 68
licence, license (US)
auxiliaire (service) (adj.) 68
ancillary
avalanche 7
avalanche, snowslide
avenue 61
avenue
avenue 61
parkway (US)
avion 50
aircraft (pl.: aircraft)
airplane, plane

B

bagages 50
baggage (US), luggage (sg.: a piece of luggage)
baie 23
bay
bain 28
bath
bains (établissement) 28
baths
bains de mer 23
bathing, sea bathing
balneothérapie 28
balneotherapy
banlieusard 61
commuter
bar 31
public bar, pub
baromètre 12
barometer
bateau 58
boat, ship (fem.)

bateau (fond transparent) 23
glass-bottom boat
Belge 77
Belgian
Belgique 77
Belgium
bénéfice 68
profit
berceau (civilisation) 45
cradle
besoin 68
need
bibliothèque 45
library
bicyclette 39
bicycle, bike
bidonville 45
shanty town
bien-aménagé / bien- equipé 17
well-appointed / well equipped, appointed (with) / equipped (with)
billet 55
ticket
billet d'avion 51
air ticket, plane ticket
billeterie 68
ticketing
Birman 77
Burmese
Birmanie 77
Burma
boissons 31
beverages, drinks
boîte aux lettres 45
mail box (US), letter box, pillar box
boîte noire 51
black box, flight recorder
Bolivie 77
Bolivia
Bolivien 77
Bolivian
bon d'échange / bon de paiement 18
voucher
bord (à) 51, 58
aboard, board (on), shipboard
bordé (de) 23
fringed (with), lined (with)
bosse 7
mogul
bouder (une destination) 68
shun (to) (a country, a destination)
boutique 83
gift shop
boutique hors-taxe 51
duty-free shops, tax-free airport shop

brèche (montagne) 7
notch
Brésil 77
Brazil
Brésilien 77
Brazilian
briller 12
shine (sun) (to), twinkle (stars) (to)
brisants 23
breakers, surf
Britannique 78
Briton (nom), British (adj.)
brochure 69
brochure, leaflet
bronzer 23
get a suntan (to), sunbathe (to)
brouillard 12
fog
bruine 12
drizzle
buffet 55
refreshment room
Bulgare 77
Bulgarian
Bulgarie 77
Bulgaria
bureau de location (théâtre, spectacles) 45
box office, ticket booth, ticket office
bureau des objets trouvés 55
lost-property office, lost and found office (US)

C

C.E.I. (Communauté d'Etats Indépendants) (ex U.R.S.S.) 78
C.I.S. (Commonwealth of Independent States) (ex USSR)
cabine 59
cabin
cabine téléphonique 45
phone booth, pay station (US), public phone
cabotage 23
coasting, coastal navigation
cadre 31
setting
cadre 35
executive
"Café- Couette" / chambre d'hôte 20
"Bed and Breakfast"
calme (adj.) 17
calm, peaceful, quiet,

tranquil, serene
calme (nom) 39
peacefulness, stillness
calmer (se) (vent, tempête...) 12
abate (to), subside (to)
Cameroun 77
Cameroon
Camerounais 77
Cameroonian
campagne 39
countryside
camper / faire du camping 39
camp (to), go camping (to)
camping (activité) 20
camping
camping-car 61
motorhome, camper, recreational vehicle, van
Canada 78
Canada
Canadien 78
Canadian
canon (à neige) 7
snow cannons
canotage 40
boating
canyon 40
canyon
cap 59
cape
capitale 46
capital, capital city
caravane 61
caravan, trailer (US)
cargo 59
cargo-boat, freighter
carte 31
à la carte menu, menu
carte (à la) 75
tailor-made
carte (de train) (abonnement général) 55
railcard, pass, railway pass, railroad pass (US)
carte d'identité 64
identity card
carte de crédit 64
credit card
carte grise 61
car licence
cascade / chutes 7
cascade / falls / waterfalls
casiers à bagages 83
baggage lockers
cathédrale 46
cathedral
caution 20
secutity bond, security deposit
ceinture de sécurité 62
seat-belt

centre commercial 46
shopping centre, shopping mall (US)
centre ville 46
inner city centre, city centre, downtown (US)
Ceylanais 81
Ceylonese
chaînes (véhicule) 7
chains, snow-chains
chalet 7, 20
chalet
chaleur 12
warmth, heat (grande chaleur)
chambre 17
bedroom, room
change 18, 83
currency exchange
change 64
exchange, foreign exchange
chariot à bagages 55
luggage trolley
chasse-neige 7
snowplough
château 20
castle, chateau (pl.: eaus/ eaux)
chaumière 20
thatched cottage
chemin 40
lane (in country), path (gén.)
chemin de grande randonnée 83
hiking trail
chemins de fer 55
railways, railroads (US)
chèques de voyage 64
traveller's cheques, traveler's checks (US)
chiffre d'affaires 69
turnover
Chili 78
Chile
Chilien 78
Chilean
Chine 78
China
Chinois 78
Chinese
chuter (températures) 12
dip (to), drop (to), fall (to)
Chypre 78
Cyprus
Chypriote 78
Cypriot (nom), Cyprian (adj)
cible 69
target
circuit 40
tour

circuit (aventure) 40
adventure holidays, adventure travel, adventure trips
circuit de distribution 69
chain of distribution
circulation 62
traffic
circuler (train) 56
run (to)
citoyen 64
citizen
classe affaires 51
business class
classe économique 51
economy class
client 31
customer, diner (restaurant), guest (pub), patron (pub)
climat 12
climate, clime
cocotier 24
coconut
code de la route 62
highway code, road regulations (US)
col (montagne) 7
pass, saddle
colline 40
hill
commande 31
order
commander 31
order (to)
commission 69
commission (uncount / count)
commission, jury 37
panel
compagnie aérienne 51
airline
compagnie de navigation 59
shipping company
compartiment 56
compartment
complet 18
fully booked, no vacancy, no vacancies
complet 51
booked up, fully booked
composter (un billet) 56
date-stamp (to) (a ticket)
comptabilité 69
accountancy, book-keeping
concurrence 69
competition
conférence 37
conference
conformer (se) (à) 65
abide (to) (by), comply (to) (with)

confort 17
comfort
confortable 17
comfortable
congrès 37
congress, convention
conseil 69
advice (uncount)
consigne (bagages) 56
left-luggage office,
baggage-room (US), locker
storage
consommation 69
consumption
consulat 65
consulate
contrat 35
contract, deal
contrôleur 56
ticket-collector
coquillages 24
seashells, shells
corail 24
coral
Corée 78
Korea
Coréen 78
Korean
correspondance 51
connection, connecting
flight
correspondance (train) 56
connection, connecting train
côte 24
coast
cottage 20
cottage
couchette (bateau) 59
berth
couvert (ciel) 12
overcast
couvrir 65
cover (to)
crépuscule 12
dusk, twilight
crête 7
ridge
crique 24
creek
crise 69
crisis, slump
critères 69
standards
croisière 59
cruise
croisière (fluviale) 40
canal cruise, river cruise,
canal cruising, river cruising
(activité)
croissance 69
growth

crustacés 24
shellfish
Cuba 78
Cuba
Cubain 78
Cuban
cuisine (art culinaire) 31
cuisine
culminer 8
soar (to), tower (to)
curatif 28
curative, healing
cure 28
cure, thermal cure
curiste 28
cure-taker, spa-goer

D

dammé(e) 8
groomed
dammer (piste) 8
groom (to)
Danemark 78
Denmark
Danois 78
Dane (nom), Danish (adj)
dater (de) 46
date back (to) (to), date (to)
(from)
débarquer 52
deplane (to), disembark, get
off the plane (to)
décalage horaire 51
jet-lag
déchiquetée (côte) 24
rugged
déclarer (douane) 65
declare (to)
décoller 51
take off (to)
découpée (côte) 24
indented
défense d'entrer 83
no entry
défense de fumer 83
no smoking
défense de stationner 83
no parking
dégâts 65
damage
dégrader 70
damage (to), spoil (to)
délégué 35
delegate, representative
demande 70
demand
demeure de caractère 21
mansion

dépasser / excéder 70
to exceed (to), top (to)
dépenses 70
expenditure, spending
**déplacer (se) (dans une ville,
un pays) 46**
get around (to), get round
(to)
dépliant 70
folder
dérailler 56
leave the metals (to), run off
the rails (to)
déréglementation 52
deregulation
dérouter (un avion) 52
divert (to), re-route (to) (a
plane)
descendre (dans un hôtel) 18
check in (to)
descendre (du train) 56
get off (the train) (to)
descendre (pente) 8
go down a slope (to),
plummet down a slope (to)
descendre des rapides 40
raft (to), run rapids (to), run
a river (to)
descendre en rappel 40
abseil (to)
dessert 32
dessert, pudding
desservir 52
link (to), serve (to)
desservir 56
call (to) (at)
destination 52
destination
destination (à) (de) 59
bound (for)
détendre (se) 40
relax (to), unwind (to)
déviation 62
detour (US), diversion
devise 65
currency
diététicien 28
dietitian
diététique (adj.) 28
dietetic
diététique (science) 28
dietetics
diminuer 70
decline, decrease, diminish
diurétique 28
diuretic
documentaire (de voyage) 70
travelogue
**documentation touristique
70**
travel data, travel literature

LEXIQUE FRANCAIS

domaine skiable 8
ski area, ski field
donner (sur) 17
overlook (to), command a
view on (to), command a
view over (to)
douane 65, 83
customs
**doux (climat, températures)
12**
mild
droit (avoir) 65
entitled (to be) (to)
**droit d'entrée (exposition,
musée, parc à thème ...) 46**
admission charge, entrance
fee
dune 24
dune
durer 35
last (to)

E

eau potable 83
drinking water
**échelonner (paiements,
vacances...) 70**
stagger (to) (payment,
holidays...)
éclaircie 13
bright interval, sunny spell
écluse 40
lock
écologie 41
ecology
**économie (d'une région ,d'un
pays ...) 70**
economy
économies 70
savings
écouteur 38
earphone
écran 38
screen
église 46
church
Egypte 78
Egypt
Egyptien 78
Egyptian
**élastique (adj.) (demande,
offre, prix) 70**
elastic (ant.: inelastic)
émaillé (de) / parsemé (de) 24
dotted (with)
embarquer 52
board (to) (a plane), embark
(to), get on (to) (a plane)

embarquer 59
board (to), embark (to), go
on board (to)
embouteillage 62
bottleneck, congestion,
tailback, traffic-jam
**emmener (quelqu'un en
voiture) 62**
give (someone) a lift (to)
en partance (pour) 59
bound (for)
encombrement (aérien) 52
air congestion, backup (US)
enjeu 71
stake
enneigement 8
snow conditions
enregistrement 18
check-in, registration
**enregistrement des bagages
83**
baggage check-in
enregistrer 18
check in (to), register (to)
enregistrer (bagages) 52
check in (to)
ensoleillé 24
sunny
entourer 24
ring (to), surround (to)
entrer dans un pays 65
enter a country (to)
époque 46
era
Equateur 78
Ecuador
Equatorien 78
Ecuadorian
équipage 52, 59
crew
équipement (de ski) 8
ski gear, ski equipment
**équipement (services,
confort) 35**
amenities
équitation 41
horse-riding
escalader 8, 41
climb (to)
escale 52
layover (US), stopover
espace aérien 53
air space
espaces verts 46
green areas, open spaces
Espagne 78
Spain
Espagnol 78
Spaniard (nom), Spanish
(adj.)
essence 62
gas (US), petrol

Etats-Unis 78
U.S.A. (United States of
America)
étendre (s') 8
stretch (to)
étendue (nom) 24
stretch
Ethiopie 78
Ethiopia
Ethiopien 78
Ethiopian
étoile 32
star
étoilé(e) 41
starlit, starry
étouffant (chaleur) 13
stifling, sultry, sweltering
étranger (adj.) 65
foreign
étude de faisabilité 71
feasability study
étude de marché 71
market research
évader (s') 41
escape (from) (to), get away
from-it-all (to)
exclure 65
exclude (to)
exercice (comptabilité) 71
financial year
exiger 66
request (to), require (to)
(usu. passive)
exploiter 74
cash in (to) (on)
exposé 37
lecture, presentation
exposition (art) 46
exhibition

F

facture 71
bill
facture 71
invoice
faire du camping 20
camping (to go)
faire du trekking 44
trek (to)
falaise 24
cliff
familiariser 71
acquaint (to) (with)
faune 41
fauna, wildlife
ferme 21, 41
farm, farmhouse
ferry 59
ferry, ferry-boat

festival 46
festival
feux autorisés 83
campfires
fiabilité, sérieux 53
reliability
financer 71
finance (to), fund (to)
Finlandais 78
Finn (nom), Finnish (adj.)
Finlande 78
Finland
fixation (ski) 8
binding
flâner 46
stroll (to)
floralies 46
flower show, horticultural
exhibition
flore 41
flora
florissant 71
booming, flourishing,
thriving
flotte aérienne 53
fleet
flux (touristique) 71
flow
forfait (ski) 8
ski-pass
formation 71
training
forme (être en) 29
fit (to be), shape (to be in),
trim (to be in)
foule 42
crowd, mob (péjoratif),
throng
frais 13
cool, fresh
frais (nom) 36
expenses, fees
Français 78
Frenchman (nom), French
(adj.)
France 78
France
**fréquentation (touristique)
71**
tourist attendance
froid 13
cold
front de mer 25
ocean-front, sea- front,
waterfront
frontière 66
border
fruits de mer 25
seafood
funiculaire 8
cable-car

fuseau horaire 53
time-zone

G

galerie (d'art) 47
art gallery
galerie marchande 47
shopping arcade
gamme / éventail 71
array (of), range (of)
garde d'enfants 18
baby-sitting service
garde forestier 42
park ranger, ranger
gare 56
station, railway station
gastronomie 32
gastronomy
gel / gelée 13
frost
gîte (rural, de montagne) 21
lodge
glacier 8
glacier
glissement de terrain 8
landslide
golf (sport) 42
golf, golfing
goûter / déguster 32
sample (to), taste (to), try
(to)
grand air, plein air 42
outdoors (nom)
Grande-Bretagne 78
Great Britain
gratte-ciel 47
skyscraper
gratuit 66
free, free of charge
Grec, Grèque 79
Greek
Grèce 79
Greece
grêle 13
hail
grill (établissement) 32
grill / steak-house
grotte 25
cave, cavern, grotto
Guatemala 79
Guatemala
Guatémaltèque 79
Guatemalan
guérir 29
cure (to), heal (to)
guichet 56
ticket office

guide 8
guide, mountain guide
guide touristique 47
guide book, touring guide,
tour book (US)
Guinée 79
Guinea
Guinéen 79
Guinean
Guyanais 79
Guyanese
Guyane 79
Guyana

H

habitant 47
dweller, inhabitant,
hameau 8
hamlet
hébergement 16
accommodation, lodging
(US)
héliporté (être) 9
airlifted (to be)
heure d'été 13
daylight saving time
heures de pointe 62
peak hours, rush hours (ant.:
slack hours)
Hollandais 79
Dutchman (nom), Dutch
(adj)
Hollande 79
Holland
Hongrie 79
Hungary
Hongrois 79
Hungarian
horaire 53, 56
schedule
horaires 56
timetable
hors-d'œuvre 32
hors-d'œuvre, starter
hostellerie 21
country house hotel,
hostelry (US)
hôtel 16
hotel
hôtel classe touriste 16
tourist class hotel
hôtel de ville 47
city hall, town hall
hôtelier (adj.) 16
hotel
hôtelier (nom) 16
hotelier, hotel-keeper
hôtesse (de l'air) 53
air-hostess, cabin attendant
(C.A.)

hôtesse (de l'air) 53
flight attendant
humide 13
humid, moist, wet

I

île 25
island
immigration 66
immigration
impasse 62
blind-alley, cul-de-sac
inclure 66
include (to)
Inde 79
India
indemnité 66
compensation (uncount),
compensation payments
indicateur 56
railway schedule, railroad
schedule (US)
Indien 79
Indian
Indonésie 79
Indonesia
Indonésien 79
Indonesian
industrie 71
industry (uncount)
informer (s') (de) 66
acquaint oneself (to) (with)
inscription 36
registration
intermédiaire (nom) 71
middleman
investissement 71
investment
inviter (quelqu'un au restaurant) 32
wine and dine (to)
(someone)
iode 25
iodine
Irak 79
Iraq
Irakien 79
Iraqi
Iran 79
Iran
Iranien 79
Iranian
Irlandais 79
Irishman (nom),
Irish (adj.)
Irlande 79
Ireland

Islandais 79
Icelander (nom), Icelandic
(adj.)
Islande 79
Iceland
Israël 79
Israel
Israëlien 79
Israeli
Italie 79
Italy
Italien 79
Italian
itinéraire 59
itinerary

J

Jamaïcain 79
Jamaican
Jamaïque 79
Jamaica
Japon 79
Japan
Japonais 80
Japanese
jardin botanique 47
botanical gardens
jardin public 47
park, public gardens
jetée 25
pier
jeux 42
games
Jordanie 80
Jordan
Jordanien 80
Jordanian
jumelage (ville) 72
town twinning

K

Kénien 80
Kenyan
Kenya 80
Kenya
kilométrage illimité 62
unlimited mileage
kiosque 56
bookstall, newsstand (US)
Koweit 80
Kuwait
Koweitien 80
Kuwaiti

L

lac 9
lake
lagon 25
lagoon
lancer un nouveau produit 72
launch a new product (to)
large (nom) 25
open sea
lèche-vitrine 47
browsing, window-
shopping
lever (se) 13
arise (to) (wind), lift (to) (fog)
liaison (aérienne) 53
airlink, link
Liban 80
Lebanon
Libanais 80
Lebanese
libérer (une chambre) 19
vacate (to) (a room)
libre (chambre) 19
vacancy, vacancies
lieu 36
venue
lieu (avoir) 36, 47
held (to be), take place (to)
lieux d'intérêt touristique 47
places of interest, places to see
ligne (d'horizon, des toits...) 47
skyline
lignes de banlieue 56
commuter lines, suburban
lines
lignes intérieures 53
domestic airlines, feeder
airlines
limitation de vitesse 62
speed limit
littoral 25
coastline, shoreline
location de voiture 83
car rental
loger 60
accommodate (to)
loi 66
law
loisirs 72
leisure (uncount)
long courrier 53
long haul
louer 21
hire (to), rent (to)
louer (véhicule) 62
rent (to)
luge (sport) 9
luge, sled (US), sledge,

toboggan
lune 13
moon
lutrin 38
lectern
Luxembourg 80
Luxemburg
Luxembourgeois 80
Luxemburger (nom),
Luxemburg (adj.)
Lybie 80
Lybia
Lybien 80
Lybian

M

**machine à traitement de
texte 38**
word processor
magnétophone 38
tape-recorder
magnétoscope 38
video-cassette-recorder (VCR)
maison à colombages 47
half-timbered house
maladie 66
disease, illness
Malais 80
Malaysian
Malaisie 80
Malaysia
Maltais 80
Maltese
Malte 80
Malta
manoir 21
manor house
marché 47, 72
market
marcher 42
hike (to), take a hike (to),
go for a walk (to), take a
walk (to), walk (to)
marée 25
tide
marin (adj.) 25
marine (adj.)
maritime 60
seafaring
Maroc 80
Morocco
Marocain 80
Moroccan
massage 29
massage
masseur 29
masseur
matériel audio-visuel 38
audio-visual equipment (AV)

Maurice 80
Mauritius
Mauricien 80
Mauritian
menu (à prix fixe) 32
table d'hôte menu, set meal
set menu,
mer 26
sea
mercatique 72
marketing
météorologie 13
meteorology
métiers du tourisme 72
careers in tourism
métro 57
undergroud, Tube (the)
(London), subway (US)
métropole 48
metropolis
mettre à (se) (+ activité) 42
take to something (to), take
to do something (to)
meublé 17
furnished
meubles 17
furniture (sg.: a piece of
furniture)
Mexicain 80
Mexican
Mexique 80
Mexico
mode 42
fashion, trend
moniteur de ski 9
ski instructor
montagne 9
mountain
monter (dans un train) 57
board (a train) (to), get on
(to) (a train) (ant.: to get off)
monument 48
monument
motel 21
motel, motorlodge
motoneige 9
snowmobile
mousson 13
monsoon, monsoon rains
moyen courrier 53
medium haul
multi-propriété 21
time-sharing
musée 48
museum

N

nationalité 66
nationality

nature 42
nature
naufrage 60
shipwreck
navette 53, 60
shuttle, shuttle bus
navette gratuite 18
courtesy coach, courtesy
shuttle
naviguer 60
sail (to)
neige 9, 13
snow, "white stuff"
neiger 13
snow (to)
Néo-zélandais 80
New Zealander
Népal 80
Nepal
Népalais 80
Nepalese
névé 9
ice-field, snow field
niché 9
nestled
niveau de vie 72
standard of living
Norvège 80
Norway
Norvégien 80
Norwegian
nourriture 32
fare, food, grub (coll)
Nouvelle-Zélande 80
New Zealand
nuage 14
cloud
nuageux 14
cloudy
numéro vert 19
freephone number, toll-free
number
nutrition 29
nutrition
nutritioniste 29
nutritionist

obèse 29
obese, overweight
objectif (nom) 72
aim, goal, objective
objets trouvés 83
lost and found
obligatoire 66
compulsory, mandatory,
obligatory
observer 43
watch (to)

office de tourisme 48
Tourist Board, Tourism Office, Convention and Visitors Bureau
opéra (bâtiment) 48
opera house
option 72
option
orage 14
thunderstorm
ordinateur 72
computer
ordinateur portable 38
laptop computer
organiser 36
organize (to), stage (to)
ouragan 14
hurricane
ouvrir (une ligne) 53
open (to) (an air route, a regular flight...), begin (to) (a new route, scheduled flights...)

P

Pakistan 80
Pakistan
Pakistanais 80
Pakistani
palmier 26
palm, palm-tree
panne 66
breakdown
panneau (signalisation) 62
road sign
panorama, point de vue 48
vista
paquebot 60
liner
paralyser 53
cripple (to)
parasol 26
umbrella
parc à thème 73
theme park
parc national 9, 43
national park
parcours 53
route
parking 18
car-park, garage facilities, parking facilities
parking 62
car park, parking-lot (US)
paroi (rocheuse) 9
cliff, wall
partir 53
depart (to), leave (to)

pass aérien 53
air pass
passager 53
passenger
passeport 66
passport
passerelle (bateau) 60
gangway
patinage (sur glace) 9
ice-skating
patinoire 9
ice rink, skating-rink
Pays-Bas 79
Netherlands (the)
paysage 43
landscape, scenery
péage 63
toll
pêcher 43
fish (to)
pêcheur 26
fisherman
péniche 43
barge
pension (de famille) 21
guest house
pente 10
slope
perdre (se) 48
get lost (to), lose one's way (to)
périphérique 63
by-pass, ring road, underpass
permis de conduire 63
driving licence, driver's licence (US)
Pérou 81
Peru
personnel (nom) 36
personnel, staff
personnel navigant 52
crew
Péruvien 81
Peruvian
petite suite 17
junior suite
phare 26, 60
lighthouse
Philippin 81
Filipino (nom), Philippine (adj.)
Philippines (les) 81
Philippines (the)
photocopieuse 38
photocopier, photocopying machine
pic 10
peak, spitz
piéton 48
pedestrian

piscine 29
pool
piste (d'envol, d'atterrissage) 54
airstrip, runway
piste (ski alpin) 10
chute, piste, slope, run
pittoresque 43, 48
picturesque, quaint, scenic
place 48
square
place (train) 57
seat
plage 26
beach
plan de ville 48
city map
plaque minéralogique 63
licence plate (US), number plate, registration plate
plat (partie du repas) 32
course
plat (récipient, mets) 32
dish
pleuvoir 14
rain (to)
plonger (avec bouteilles) 26
scuba-dive (to)
plonger (gén.) 26
dive (to)
plonger (sans bouteilles) 26
skin-dive (to) (= to snorkel)
pluie 14
rain
pluvieux 14
rainy
point de vue 83
viewing area
politique touristique 73
tourist policy
Pologne 81
Poland
Polonais 81
Pole (nom), Polish (adj.)
ponctualité 54
ponctuality
pont 48
bridge
pont (bateau) 60
deck
port 26, 60
harbour, port
Portugais 81
Portuguese
Portugal 81
Portugal
posséder (être fier de..., se vanter de...) 48
boast (to)
poste 48
post office

poste de secours 26
first-aid hut, first aid
pouponnière 83
nursery
pourboire 32
gratuity, tip
pouvoir d'achat 73
purchasing power, spending
capacity (US)
**prendre le train (pour se
rendre à son travail) 57**
commute (to)
presqu'île 27
peninsula
prestataire de service 73
service provider, service
supplier
prêt (nom) (somme prêtée) 73
loan
prévention 29
prevention
prévoir 73
forecast (to), foresee (to),
predict (to)
prix / tarifs 73
fares, prices, rates
produit 73
product
produit intérieur brut (PIB) 73
gross domestic product
(GDP)
professionnel (adj.) 73
professional
profiter (de) 74
capitalize (to) (on)
programme 36
programme, program (US)
projecteur de diapositives 38
slide projector
promontoire 27
headland, promontory
promouvoir 74
foster (to), promote (to)
proposer 33
feature (to)
protéger 43
protect (to)
publicité (gén.) 74
advertising

Q

quai (bateau) 60
quay, wharf (pl.: wharves)
quai (train) 57
platform
quarantaine 67
quarantine, quarantine period
quartier 48
area, district, neighborhood

(US)
quasi-collision 54
near-miss
quitter (un hôtel) 19
check out (to)
quitter la gare (train) 57
depart from the station (to),
leave the station (to),
pull out of the station (to)

R

rafale 14
blizzard (snow), gust (wind)
ranch 21
ranch
randonnée 43
ramble, rambling (activité)
raquette (montagne) 10
snowshoe
recettes 74
receipts
recherche 74
research (uncount)
récif 27
reef
recommander 33
recommend (to)
refuge 10
mountain hut
régime 29
diet
réglementation 67
regulation(s)
règlementation / règlement 54
regulations / rules
relais 21
country inn, countryside inn
relié (à) 74
connected (with), linked (to,
with)
relier 57
connect (to), link (to)
rembourser 74
refund (to)
remonte-pente 10
lift, ski lift, tow, ski-tow
remparts 49
ramparts, walls
renommé / réputé 33
celebrated, famed, famous
renowned, well-known
renseignements hôteliers 83
hotel information
rentable 74
profitable
repas 33
meals
répertorier 21
list (to)

répondre aux exigences 75
meet demands (to)
repos 29
relaxation, rest
représenter 75
account (to) (for)
réputation 75
reputation
réseau (ferroviaire) 57
network (railway)
réseau routier 63
road network
réservation 19, 36, 75
booking
reservation
réserve 43
reserve, wildlife park
réserver (une table) 33
book (to) (a table)
restaurant 33
eatery (US), eating place
(US), dining spot, restaurant
restriction 67
restriction
retardé 57
delayed, late
retarder (un vol) 54
delay (to) (a flight)
retrait des bagages 83
baggage claim, luggage claim
réunion 38
meeting
revenu 75
income, revenue
revitalisant 29
rejuvenating
rivage 27
shore
rive 10
bank (river), shore (lake)
rouler (avion) 54
taxi (to)
Roumain 81
Romanian
Roumanie 81
Romania, Rumania
route 63
road
route des fromages 43
cheese route
route des vins 43
wine route
rue 49
street

S

sain 29
healthy

LEXIQUE FRANCAIS

saison 14, 75
season
salle d'attente 57
waiting-room
salle de conférence 36
conference room
salon (foire, exposition) 36
exhibition, fair, trade-fair
salon (hôtel, aéroport) 37
lounge
salon de thé 33
coffee-shop, tea-shop
salon des antiquaires 49
antiques fair
santé 29, 67
health
Saoudien 77
Saudi Arabian
sauna 29
sauna
sauver 10, 61
rescue (to)
sec / sècheresse 14
dry / drought
sécurité 54
safety, security
séminaire 38
seminar
Sénégal 81
Senegal
Sénégalais 81
Senegalese
sentier 44
footpath, trail
serveur(euse) 33
waiter(ress)
service 33
service
Seychelles (les) 81
Seychelles (the)
Seychellois 81
Seychellois
Singapour 81
Singapore
Singapourien 81
Singaporean
situé 22
located, set, situated
situé (être) 27
lie (to), located (to be), set
(to be), situated (to be)
skier 10
ski (to), take to the slopes (to)
sol (au) 54
ground (on the)
solde (comptabilité) 75
balance
soleil 14, 27
sun, sunshine
Somalie 81
Somalia

Somalien 81
Somali (nom), Somalian (adj.)
sommelier 33
wine-waiter
sommet 10
peak, summit, top
sortie de secours 54
emergency exit
Soudan 81
Sudan (the)
Soudanais 81
Sudanese
soulager 29
relieve (to)
source 30
spa, spring
sous-marin (adj.) 27
underwater
spécialité 33
speciality, speciality dish
spéléologie 44
potholing, spelunking (US)
sport (s) 44
sport (s)
sports d'hiver 11
winter sports
sports nautiques 27
aquatic sports, watersports
Sri Lanka (ex-Ceylan) 81
Sri Lanka (ex-Ceylon)
station balnéaire 27
sea resort, seaside resort
station climatique 30
health resort
station de ski 11
ski resort, skiing resort,
winter resort
station thermale 30
spa, spa-town, thermal resort
style contemporain 49
contemporary
style gothique 49
gothic
style moyenâgeux 49
medieval
style renaissance 49
renaissance
style roman 49
romanesque
subventions 75
subsidies
Sud-Africain 77
South African
Suède 81
Sweden
Suédois 81
Swede (nom), Swedish
(adj.)
Suisse 81
Switzerland, Swiss,

suite 17
suite
suite de luxe 17
luxury, penthouse suite
supplément 57
excess fare
supprimer 54
cancel (a flight) (to),
discontinue (to)(an airlink)
sur-mesure 75
tailor-made
surpeuplé 49
cramped, overcrowded
surplomber 27
overlook (to) (something),
jut above (to) (something),
jut over (to) (something)
symposium (pl.: symposia) 38
symposium
syndicat d'initiative 49
tourist information centre,
visitor information center (US)
Syrie 81
Syria
Syrien 81
Syrian

T

T.V.A. 34
V.A.T. (value added tax)
table d'hôte 34
table d'hôte, set meal service
tarif 54
fare, rate
taux d'occupation (d'un hôtel) 19
occupancy rate
taxe 75
tax
taxe de séjour 19
residence tax (US), sejourn tax
taxi 63
cab, taxi, taxicab
télécopieur 38
fax machine
télésiège 11
chair lift
téléski 11
skilift, T-bar
température 14
temperature
tempéré 14
temperate
tempête 14
storm
temps 14
weather
tenir un hôtel 16
manage a hotel (to), run a

hotel (to)
terre (à) 61
ashore, on-shore
Thaïlandais 81
Thai
Thaïlande 81
Thailand
théâtre 49
theatre, theater (US)
thérapeutique (adj.) 30
therapeutic
thérapie 30
therapy
thermal 30
thermal
thermes 30
thermae
Tibet 81
Tibet
Tibétain 81
Tibetan
titre de transport 54
ticket
toilettes 83
toilets, restrooms (US)
torrent 11
stream, mountain stream
tourisme de loisirs 75
recreational tourism
tourisme fluvial 44
inland waterway tourism
tourisme vert 44
"green" holiday, "green"
vacations (US)
trafic aérien 54
air-traffic
train 57
train
traîneau 11
sleigh
traitement 30
treatment
traitement de faveur 37
red-carpet treatment
**tranquille (allure,
mouvement) 44**
leisurely (pace, movement)
transfert 54
transfer
transporter (passagers) 54
carry (to) (passengers)
transporteur aérien 55
carrier, air carrier
transports en commun 63
public transport
traversée (maritime) 60
crossing, sea-crossing,
voyage
trekking 44
trekking

Tunisie 82
Tunisia
Tunisien 82
Tunisian
turbulence 55
turbulence (uncount)
Turc (nom) 82
Turk (nom)
Turque (adj.) 82
Turkish (adj.)
Turquie 82
Turkey
typhon 14
typhoon

U

université 49
college, university
urbanisme 49
town-planning
Uruguay 82
Uruguay
Uruguayen 82
Uruguayan

V

vacances 76
holidays, vacations (US)
vacances actives 44
action-packed holidays,
activity holidays (ant.:
passive vacationing)
vacances originales 44
holidays with a difference,
unusual holidays
vaccination 67
inoculation, vaccination
vague 27
wave
vaincre (un sommet) 11
conquer (a peak) (to)
vallée 11
valley
Vénézuela 82
Venezuela
Vénézuelien 82
Venezuelan
vent 15, 27
wind
vêtements de ski 11
skiwear
vierge (intact, pas défiguré) 27
unspoilt, unspoiled
Vietnam 82
Vietnam

Vietnamien 82
Vietnamese
vigueur (en) 67
force (in)
ville 49
city, town
**vin (blanc, pétillant, rosé,
rouge...) 34**
wine (white, sparkling, rosé,
red...)
virage 63
bend, curve
visa 67
visa
visite (d'une ville) 49
sightseeing tour, tour
vivre du tourisme 76
live off tourism (to)
voies navigables 61
inland waterways
voilier 27
sailing-boat
vol 55
flight
volcan 11
volcano (pl.: volcanoes)
volonté (à) 34
unlimited
voyage 76
journey, trip, voyage
voyager en train 58
ride a train (to),
travel by train (to)
voyages de stimulation 37
incentive travel (uncount),
incentive trips

W - Y

wagon 58
carriage, car (US), coach
railcar (US)
Yougoslave 82
Yugoslav (nom),
Yugoslavian (adj.)
Yougoslavie 82
Yugoslavia
Zaïre 82
Zaire
Zaïrois 82
Zairean
zone de jeux 83
playground
zone fumeur 55
smoking area
zone non-fumeur 55
no-smoking area, non-
smoking area

LEXIQUE ANGLAIS

A

à la carte menu 31
carte
abate (to) 12
calmer (se) (vent, tempête...)
abbey 45
abbatiale, abbaye
abide (to) (by) 65
conformer (se) (à)
aboard 51, 58
bord (à)
abseil (to) 40
descendre en rappel
accommodate (to) 60
loger
accommodation 16
hébergement
account (to) (for) 75
représenter
accountancy 69
comptabilité
acquaint (to) (with) 71
familiariser
acquaint oneself (to) (with) 66
informer (s') (de)
action-packed holidays 44
vacances actives
**activity holidays (ant.:
passive vacationing) 44**
vacances actives
admission charge 46
droit d'entrée (exposition,
musée, parc à thème ...)
adventure holidays 40
circuit (aventure)
adventure travel 40
circuit (aventure)
adventure trips 40
circuit (aventure)
advertising 74
publicité (gén.)
advice (uncount) 69
conseil
affliction 28
affection
Afghan 77
Afghan
Afghanistan 77
Afghanistan

after-ski 7
après-ski
ailment, trouble 28
affection
aim 72
objectif (nom)
air carrier 55
transporteur aérien
air congestion 52
encombrement (aérien)
air pass 53
pass aérien
air space 53
espace aérien
air ticket 51
billet d'avion
air-hostess 53
hôtesse (de l'air)
air-traffic 54
trafic aérien
aircraft (pl.: aircraft) 50
avion
airfield 50
aérodrome
airlifted (to be) 9
héliporté (être)
airline 51
compagnie aérienne
airlink 53
liaison (aérienne)
airplane 50
avion
airport 50
aéroport
airstrip 54
piste (d'envol, d'atterrissage)
· Algeria 77
Algérie
Algerian 77
Algérien
allocate (to) 68
allouer
alluring 68
attirant
amenities 35
équipement (services, confort)
American 78
Américain
anchor 58
ancre

ancillary 68
auxiliaire (service) (adj.)
antiques fair 49
salon des antiquaires
apartment (US) 19
appartement
appetizer 31
amuse-gueule
aquatic sports 27
sports nautiques
archipelago 23
archipel
architecture 45
architecture
area 48
quartier
Argentina 77
Argentine
Argentinian 77
Argentin
arise (to) (wind) 13
lever (se)
array (of) 71
gamme / éventail
art gallery 47
galerie (d'art)
ashore 61
terre (à)
asset 45
atout
atoll 23
atoll
attractive 68
attirant
audio-visual equipment (AV) 38
matériel audio-visuel
auditorium 37
auditorium
Australia 77
Australie
Australian 77
Australien
avalanche 7
avalanche
avenue 61
avenue

B

baby-sitting service 18
 garde d'enfants
backup (US) 52
 encombrement (aérien)
baggage (US) 50
 bagages
baggage check-in 83
 enregistrement des bagages
baggage claim 83
 retrait des bagages
baggage lockers 83
 caziers à bagages
baggage-room (US) 56
 consigne (bagages)
balance 75
 solde (comptabilité)
ballooning 39
 ascencion en ballon
balneotherapy 28
 balneothérapie
bank (river) 10
 rive
barge 43
 péniche
barometer 12
 baromètre
bath 28
 bain
bathing 23
 bains de mer
baths 28
 bains (établissement)
bay 23
 baie
beach 26
 plage
"Bed and Breakfast" 20
 "Café- Couette" / chambre
 d'hôte
bedroom 17
 chambre
beekeeper 39
 apiculteur
beekeeping 39
 apiculture
**begin (to) (a new route,
scheduled flights...) 53**
 ouvrir (une ligne)
Belgian 77
 Belge
Belgium 77
 Belgique
bend 63
 virage
berth 59
 couchette (bateau)
beverages 31
 boissons
bicycle 39
 bicyclette
bike 39
 bicyclette

bill 31
 addition
bill 71
 facture
binding 8
 fixation (ski)
black box 51
 boîte noire
blind-alley 62
 impasse
blizzard (snow) 14
 rafale
board (a train) (to) 57
 monter (dans un train)
board (on) 51, 58
 bord (à)
board (to) 59
 embarquer
board (to) (a plane) 52
 embarquer
boast (to) 48
 posséder (être fier de..., se
 vanter de...)
boat 58
 bateau
boating 40
 canotage
Bolivia 77
 Bolivie
Bolivian 77
 Bolivien
book (to) (a table) 33
 réserver (une table)
book-keeping 69
 comptabilité
booked up 51
 complet
booking 19, 36, 75
 réservation
bookstall 56
 kiosque
booming 71
 florissant
border 66
 frontière
botanical gardens 47
 jardin botanique
bottleneck 62
 embouteillage
bound (for) 59
 à destination (de),
 en partance (pour)
box office 45
 bureau de location (théâtre,
 spectacles)
Brazil 77
 Brésil
Brazilian 77
 Brésilien
breakdown 66
 panne
breakers 23
 brisants
bridge 48
 pont

bright interval 13
 éclaircie
British (adj.) 78
 Britannique
Briton (nom) 78
 Britannique
brochure 69
 brochure
browsing 47
 lèche-vitrine
Bulgaria 77
 Bulgarie
Bulgarian 77
 Bulgare
Burma 77
 Birmanie
Burmese 77
 Birman
bus 45
 autobus (urbain)
business 35
 affaires
business class 51
 classe affaires
bustling 45
 animé
by-pass 63
 périphérique

C

**C.I.S. (Commonwealth of
Independent States) (ex
USSR) 78**
 C.E.I. (Communauté d'Etats
 Indépendants) (ex U.R.S.S.)
cab 63
 taxi
cabin 59
 cabine
cabin attendant (C.A.) 53
 hôtesse (de l'air)
cable-car 8
 funiculaire
call (to) (at) 56
 desservir
calm 17
 calme (adj.)
Cameroon 77
 Cameroun
Cameroonian 77
 Camerounais
camp (to) 39
 camper / faire du camping
camper 61
 camping-car
campfires 83
 feux autorisés
camping 20
 camping (activité)
camping (to go) 20
 faire du camping

LEXIQUE ANGLAIS

Canada 78
Canada
Canadian 78
Canadien
canal cruise, river cruise 40
croisière (fluviale)
canal cruising, river cruising (activité) 40
croisière (fluviale)
cancel (a flight) (to) 54
supprimer
cancel (to) 18
annuler
cancel (to) 50
annuler (une réservation, un vol)
cancellation 18
annulation
canyon 40
canyon
cape 59
cap
capital 46
capitale
capital city 46
capitale
capitalize (to) (on) 74
profiter (de)
car (US) 58
wagon
car licence 61
carte grise
car park 18, 62
parking
car rental 83
location de voiture
caravan 61
caravane
careers in tourism 72
métiers du tourisme
cargo-boat 59
cargo
carriage 58
wagon
carrier 55
transporteur aérien
carry (to) (passengers) 54
transporter (passagers)
cascade / falls / waterfalls 7
cascade / chutes
cash in (to) (on) 74
exploiter
castle 20
château
cathedral 46
cathédrale
cave 25
grotte
cavern 25
grotte
celebrated 33
renommé / reputé
Ceylonese 81
Ceylanais

chain of distribution 69
circuit de distribution
chains 7
chaînes (véhicule)
chair lift 11
télésiège
chalet 7, 20
chalet
charter (to) (a plane) 50
affréter (un avion)
chateau (pl.: eaus/eaux) 20
château
check in (to) 18
descendre (dans un hôtel),
enregistrer
check in (to) 52
enregistrer (bagages)
check out (to) 19
quitter (un hôtel)
check (US) 31
addition
check-in 18
enregistrement
cheese route 43
route des fromages
Chile 78
Chili
Chilean 78
Chilien
China 78
Chine
Chinese 78
Chinois
church 46
église
chute 10
piste (ski alpin)
citizen 64
citoyen
city 49
ville
city centre 46
centre ville
city hall 47
hôtel de ville
city map 48
plan de ville
cliff 9
paroi (rocheuse)
cliff 24
falaise
climate 12
climat
climb (to) 8, 41
escalader
clime 12
climat
cloud 14
nuage
cloudy 14
nuageux
coach 45
autobus (inter-urbain)
coach 58
wagon

coast 24
côte
coastal development 23
aménagement du littoral
coastal navigation 23
cabotage
coasting 23
cabotage
coastline 25
littoral
coconut 24
cocotier
coffee-shop 33
salon de thé
cold 13
froid
college 49
université
come alongside (to) 58
accoster
comfort 17
confort
comfortable 17
confortable
command a view on (to) 17
donner (sur)
command a view over (to) 17
donner (sur)
commission (uncount/count) 69
commission
community hotel (cotel, US) 20
auberge de jeunesse
commute (to) 57
prendre le train (pour se rendre à son travail)
commuter 61
banlieusard
commuter lines 56
lignes de banlieue
compartment 56
compartiment
compensation (uncount) 66
indemnité
compensation payments 66
indemnité
competition 69
concurrence
comply (to) (with) 65
conformer (se) (à)
compulsory 66
obligatoire
computer 72
ordinateur
conference 37
conférence
conference room 36
salle de conférence
congestion 62
embouteillage
congress 37
congrès
connect (to) 57
relier

connected (with) 74
relié (à)
connecting flight 51
correspondance
connecting train 56
correspondance (train)
connection 51, 56
correspondance
conquer (a peak) (to) 11
vaincre (un sommet)
consulate 65
consulat
consumption 69
consommation
contemporary 49
style contemporain
contract 35
contrat
convention 37
congrès
cool 13
frais
coral 24
corail
cottage 20
cottage
country house hotel 21
hostellerie
country inn 21
relais
country inn 31
auberge
countryside 39
campagne
countryside inn 21
relais
courier 68
accompagnateur
course 32
plat (partie du repas)
courtesy coach 18
navette gratuite
courtesy shuttle 18
navette gratuite
cove 23
anse
cover (to) 65
couvrir
cradle 45
berceau (civilisation)
cramped 49
surpeuplé
credit card 64
carte de crédit
creek 24
crique
crew 52, 59
équipage, personnel
navigant
cripple (to) 53
paralyser
crisis 69
crise
crossing 60
traversée (maritime)

crowd 42
foule
cruise 59
croisière
Cuba 78
Cuba
Cuban 78
Cubain
cuisine 31
cuisine (art culinaire)
cul-de-sac 62
impasse
curative 28
curatif
cure 28
cure
cure (to) 29
guérir
cure-taker 28
curiste
currency 65
devise
currency exchange 18, 83
change
curve 63
virage
customer 31
client
customs 65
douane
customs 83
douane
Cyprian (adj) 78
Chypriote
Cypriot (nom) 78
Chypriote
Cyprus 78
Chypre

D

damage 65
dégâts
damage (to) 70
dégrader
Dane (nom) 78
Danois
Danish (adj) 78
Danois
date (to) (from) 46
dater (de)
date back (to) (to) 46
dater (de)
date-stamp (to) (a ticket) 56
composter (un billet)
dawn 12
aube
daylight saving time 13
heure d'été
deal 35
contrat
deck 60
pont (bateau)

declare (to) 65
déclarer (douane)
decline 70
diminuer
decrease 70
diminuer
delay (to) (a flight) 54
retarder (un vol)
delayed 57
retardé
delegate 35
délégué
demand 70
demande
Denmark 78
Danemark
depart (to) 53
partir
depart from the station (to) 57
quitter la gare (train)
deplane (to) 52
débarquer
deposit 18
arrhes
deregulation 52
déréglementation
dessert 32
dessert
destination 52
destination
detour (US) 62
déviation
diet 29
régime
dietetic 28
diététique (adj.)
dietetics 28
diététique (science)
dietitian 28
diététicien
diminish 70
diminuer
diner (restaurant) 31
client
dining spot 33
restaurant
dip (to) 12
chuter (températures)
discontinue (to)(an airlink) 54
supprimer
disease 66
maladie
disembark 52
débarquer
dish 32
plat (récipient, mets)
district 48
quartier
diuretic 28
diurétique
dive (to) 26
plonger (gén.)

diversion 62
déviation
divert (to) 52
dérouter (un avion)
domestic airlines 53
lignes intérieures
dotted (with) 24
émaillé (de) / parsemé (de)
downtown (US) 46
centre ville
draw 45
atout
drawing card 45
atout
drinking water 83
eau potable
drinks 31
boissons
driver's licence (US) 63
permis de conduire
driving licence 63
permis de conduire
drizzle 12
bruine
drop (to) 12
chuter (températures)
dry / drought 14
sec / sècheresse
dune 24
dune
dusk 12
crépuscule
Dutch (adj) 79
Hollandais
Dutchman (nom) 79
Hollandais
duty-free shops 51
boutique hors-taxe
dweller 47
habitant

E

earphone 38
écouteur
eatery (US) 33
restaurant
eating place (US) 33
restaurant
ecology 41
écologie
economy 70
économie (d'une région,
d'un pays ...)
economy class 51
classe économique
Ecuador 78
Equateur
Ecuadorian 78
Equatorien
Egypt 78
Egypte

Egyptian 78
Egyptien
elastic (ant.: inelastic) 70
élastique (adj.) (demande,
offre, prix)
elevation 7
altitude
elevator(US) 18
ascenseur
embark (to) 52, 59
embarquer
embassy 64
ambassade
emergency exit 54
sortie de secours
enter a country (to) 65
entrer dans un pays
entitled (to be) (to) 65
droit (avoir)
entrance fee 46
droit d'entrée (exposition,
musée, parc à thème ...)
era 46
époque
escape (from) (to) 41
évader (s')
Ethiopia 78
Ethiopie
Ethiopian 78
Ethiopien
exceed (to) 70
dépasser / excéder
excess fare 57
supplément
exchange 64
change
exclude (to) 65
exclure
executive 35
cadre
exhibition 36
salon (foire, exposition)
exhibition 46
exposition (art)
expenditure 70
dépenses
expenses 36
frais (nom)

F

facilities for the disabled 18
aménagements pour les
handicapés
**facilities for the handicapped
18**
aménagements pour les
handicapés
fair 36
salon (foire, exposition)
fall (to) 12
chuter (températures)

famed 33
renommé / reputé
famous 33
renommé / reputé
fare 32
nourriture
fare 54, 73
tarif, prix
farm 21, 41
ferme
farmhouse 21, 41
ferme
fashion 42
mode
fauna 41
faune
fax machine 38
télécopieur
feasability study 71
étude de faisabilité
feature (to) 33
proposer
feeder airlines 53
lignes intérieures
fees 36
frais (nom)
ferry 59
ferry
ferry-boat 59
ferry
festival 46
festival
Filipino (nom) 81
Philippin
finance (to) 71
financer
financial year 71
exercice (comptabilité)
fine 61
amende
Finland 78
Finlande
Finn (nom) 78
Finlandais
Finnish (adj.) 78
Finlandais
first aid 83
poste de secours
first-aid hut 26
poste de secours
fish (to) 43
pêcher
fisherman 26
pêcheur
fit (to be) 29
forme (être en)
flat 19
appartement
fleet 53
flotte aérienne
flight 55
vol
flight attendant 53
hôtesse (de l'air)

flight recorder 51
boîte noire
flora 41
flore
flourishing 71
florissant
flow 71
flux (touristique)
flower show 46
floralies
fog 12
brouillard
folder 70
dépliant
food 32
nourriture
footpath 44
sentier
force (in) 67
vigueur (en)
forecast (to) 73
prévoir
foreign 65
étranger (adj.)
foreign exchange 64
change
foresee (to) 73
prévoir
foster (to) 74
promouvoir
France 78
France
free 66
gratuit
free of charge 66
gratuit
freephone number 19
numéro vert
freighter 59
cargo
French (adj.) 78
Français
Frenchman (nom) 78
Français
fresh 13
frais
fringed (with) 23
bordé (de)
frost 13
gel / gelée
fully booked 18, 51
complet
fund (to) 71
financer
furnished 17
meublé
furniture (sg.: a piece of furniture) 17
meubles

G

games 42
jeux
gangway 60
passerelle (bateau)
garage facilities 18
parking
gas (US) 62
essence
gastronomy 32
gastronomie
German 77
Allemand
Germany 77
Allemagne
get a suntan (to) 23
bronzer
get around (to) 46
déplacer (se) (dans une ville, un pays)
get away from-it-all (to) 41
évader (s')
get lost (to) 48
perdre (se)
get off (the train) (to) 56
descendre (du train)
get off the plane (to) 52
débarquer
get on (to) (a plane) 52
embarquer
get on (to) (a train) (ant.: to get off) 57
monter (dans un train)
get round (to) 46
déplacer (se) (dans une ville, un pays)
get under way (to) 58
appareiller (bateau)
gift shop 83
boutique
give (someone) a lift (to) 62
emmener (quelqu'un en voiture)
glacier 8
glacier
glass-bottom boat 23
bateau (fond transparent)
go camping (to) 39
camper / faire du camping
go down a slope (to) 8
descendre (pente)
go for a walk (to) 42
marcher
go on board (to) 59
embarquer
goal 72
objectif (nom)
golf 42
golf (sport)
golfing 42
golf (sport)
gothic 49
style gothique

gratuity 32
pourboire
Great Britain 78
Grande-Bretagne
Greece 79
Grèce
Greek 79
Grec, Grèque
green areas 46
espaces verts
"green" holiday 44
tourisme vert
"green" vacations (US) 44
tourisme vert
grill / steak-house 32
grill (établissement)
groom (to) 8
dammer (piste)
groomed 8
dammé(e)
gross domestic product (GDP) 73
produit intérieur brut (PIB)
grotto 25
grotte
ground (on the) 54
sol (au)
growth 69
croissance
grub (coll) 32
nourriture
Guatemala 79
Guatemala
Guatemalan 79
Guatémaltèque
guest (pub) 31
client
guest house 21
pension (de famille)
guide 8
guide
guide book 47
guide touristique
Guinea 79
Guinée
Guinean 79
Guinéen
gust (wind) 14
rafale
Guyana 79
Guyane
Guyanese 79
Guyanais

H

hail 13
grêle
half-timbered house 47
maison à colombages
hamlet 8
hameau

harbour 26, 60
port
headland 27
promontoire
heal (to) 29
guérir
healing 28
curatif
health 29, 67
santé
health resort 30
station climatique
healthy 29
sain
heat (grande chaleur) 12
chaleur
held (to be) (at, in) 36, 47
lieu (avoir)
highway code 62
code de la route
hike (to) 42
marcher
hiking trail 83
chemin de grande randonnée
hill 40
colline
hinterland (nom) 39
arrière-pays
hire (to) 21
louer
hitch-hiker 61
auto-stoppeur
holidays 76
vacances
holidays with a difference 44
vacances originales
Holland 79
Hollande
hors-d'œuvre 32
hors-d'œuvre
horse-riding 41
équitation
horticultural exhibition 46
floralies
hostel 20
auberge de jeunesse
hostelry (US) 21
hostellerie
hotel 16
hôtel, hôtelier (adj.)
hotel information 83
renseignements hôteliers
hotel-keeper 16
hôtelier (nom)
hotelier 16
hôtelier (nom)
hovercraft 58
aéroglisseur
humid 13
humide
Hungarian 79
Hongrois
Hungary 79
Hongrie

hurricane 14
ouragan

I

ice rink, skating-rink 9
patinoire
ice-field 9
névé
ice-skating 9
patinage (sur glace)
Iceland 79
Islande
Icelander (nom) 79
Islandais
Icelandic (adj.) 79
Islandais
identity card 64
carte d'identité
illness 66
maladie
immigration 66
immigration
incentive travel (uncount) 37
voyages de stimulation
incentive trips 37
voyages de stimulation
include (to) 66
inclure
income 75
revenu
indented 24
découpée (côte)
India 79
Inde
Indian 79
Indien
Indonesia 79
Indonésie
Indonesian 79
Indonésien
industry (uncount) 71
industrie
influx 68
affluence (touristique)
inhabitant 47
habitant
inland waterway tourism 44
tourisme fluvial
inland waterways 61
voies navigables
inn 20, 31
auberge
inner city centre 46
centre ville
inoculation 67
vaccination
insurance 61
assurance
insurance (uncount) 64
assurance
investment 71
investissement

invoice 71
facture
iodine 25
iode
Iran 79
Iran
Iranian 79
Iranien
Iraq 79
Irak
Iraqi 79
Irakien
Ireland 79
Irlande
Irish (adj.) 79
Irlandais
Irishman (nom) 79
Irlandais
island 25
île
Israel 79
Israël
Israeli 79
Israëlien
Italian 79
Italien
Italy 79
Italie
itinerary 59
itinéraire

J

Jamaica 79
Jamaïque
Jamaican 79
Jamaïcain
Japan 79
Japon
Japanese 80
Japonais
jet-lag 51
décalage horaire
Jordan 80
Jordanie
Jordanian 80
Jordanien
journey 76
voyage
junior suite 17
petite suite
jut above (to) (something) 27
surplomber
jut over (to) (something) 27
surplomber

K

Kenya 80
Kenya
Kenyan 80
Kénien

Korea 78
Corée
Korean 78
Coréen
Kuwait 80
Koweit
Kuwaiti 80
Koweitien

L

lagoon 25
lagon
lake 9
lac
land (to) 50
atterrir
landscape 43
paysage
landslide 8
glissement de terrain
lane (in country) 40
chemin
laptop computer 38
ordinateur portable
last (to) 35
durer
late 57
retardé
launch a new product (to) 72
lancer un nouveau produit
law 66
loi
layover (US) 52
escale
leaflet 69
brochure
leave (to) 53
partir
leave the metals (to) 56
dérailler
leave the station (to) 57
quitter la gare (train)
Lebanese 80
Libanais
Lebanon 80
Liban
lectern 38
lutrin
lecture 37
exposé
left-luggage office 56
consigne (bagages)
leisure (uncount) 72
loisirs
leisurely (pace, movement) 44
tranquille (allure, mouvement)
letter box 45
boîte aux lettres
library 45
bibliothèque

licence 68
autorisation / permis
licence plate (US) 63
plaque minéralogique
license (US) 68
autorisation / permis
lie (to) 27
situé (être)
lift 10
remonte-pente
lift 18
ascenseur
lift (to) (fog) 13
lever (se)
lighthouse 26, 60
phare
lined (with) 23
bordé (de)
liner 60
paquebot
link 53
liaison (aérienne)
link (to) 52
desservir
link (to) 57
relier
linked (to, with) 74
relié (à)
list (to) 21
répertorier
live off tourism (to) 76
vivre du tourisme
lively 45
animé
loan 73
prêt (nom) (somme prêtée)
located 22
situé
located (to be) 27
situé (être)
lock 40
écluse
locker storage 56
consigne (bagages)
lodge 21
gîte (rural, de montagne)
lodging (US) 16
hébergement
long haul 53
long courrier
lose one's way (to) 48
perdre (se)
lost and found 83
objets trouvés
lost and found office (US) 55
bureau des objets trouvés
lost-property office 55
bureau des objets trouvés
lounge 37
salon (hôtel, aéroport)
luge 9
luge (sport)
luggage (sg.: a piece of luggage) 50
bagages

luggage claim 83
retrait des bagages
luggage trolley 55
chariot à bagages
lure 45
attrait
Luxemburg 80
Luxembourg
Luxemburg (adj.) 80
Luxembourgeois
Luxemburger (nom) 80
Luxembourgeois
luxury 17
suite de luxe
Lybia 80
Lybie
Lybian 80
Lybien

M

mail box (US) 45
boîte aux lettres
main thoroughfare 61
artère principale
Malaysia 80
Malaisie
Malaysian 80
Malais
Malta 80
Malte
Maltese 80
Maltais
manage a hotel (to) 16
tenir un hôtel
mandatory 66
obligatoire
manor house 21
manoir
mansion 21
demeure de caractère
marine (adj.) 25
marin (adj.)
market 47, 72
marché
market research 71
étude de marché
marketing 72
mercatique
massage 29
massage
masseur 29
masseur
Mauritian 80
Mauricien
Mauritius 80
Maurice
meals 33
repas
medieval 49
style moyenâgeux
medium haul 53
moyen courrier

meet demands (to) 75
  répondre aux exigences
meeting 38
  réunion
menu 31
  carte
meteorology 13
  météorologie
metropolis 48
  métropole
Mexican 80
  Mexicain
Mexico 80
  Mexique
middleman 71
  intermédiaire (nom)
mild 12
  doux (climat, températures)
mob (péjoratif) 42
  foule
mogul 7
  bosse
moist 13
  humide
monsoon 13
  mousson
monsoon rains 13
  mousson
monument 48
  monument
moon 13
  lune
Moroccan 80
  Marocain
Morocco 80
  Maroc
motel 21
  motel
motorhome 61
  camping-car
motorlodge 21
  motel
mountain 9
  montagne
mountain guide 8
  guide
mountain hut 10
  refuge
mountain landing strip 7
  altipiste / altiport
mountain stream 11
  torrent
mountain-climbing 7
  alpinisme
mountaineering 7
  alpinisme
museum 48
  musée

N

national park 9, 43
  parc national

nationality 66
  nationalité
nature 42
  nature
near-miss 54
  quasi-collision
need 68
  besoin
neighborhood (US) 48
  quartier
Nepal 80
  Népal
Nepalese 80
  Népalais
nestled 9
  niché
Netherlands (the) 79
  Pays-Bas
network (railway) 57
  réseau (ferroviaire)
New Zealand 80
  Nouvelle-Zélande
New Zealander 80
  Néo-zélandais
newsstand (US) 56
  kiosque
no entry 83
  défense d'entrer
no parking 83
  défense de stationner
no smoking 83
  défense de fumer
no vacancies 18
  complet
no vacancy 18
  complet
no-smoking area 55
  zone non-fumeur
non-smoking area 55
  zone non-fumeur
Norway 80
  Norvège
Norwegian 80
  Norvégien
notch 7
  brèche (montagne)
number plate 63
  plaque minéralogique
nursery 83
  pouponnière
nutrition 29
  nutrition
nutritionist 29
  nutritioniste

O

obese 29
  obèse
objective 72
  objectif (nom)
obligatory 66
  obligatoire

occupancy rate 19
  taux d'occupation (d'un hôtel)
ocean-front 25
  front de mer
on-shore 61
  terre (à)
open (to) (an air route, a regular flight...) 53
  ouvrir (une ligne)
open sea 25
  large (nom)
open spaces 46
  espaces verts
opera house 48
  opéra (bâtiment)
option 72
  option
order 31
  commande
order (to) 31
  commander
organize (to) 36
  organiser
outdoors (nom) 42
  grand air, plein air
overcast 12
  couvert (ciel)
overcrowded 49
  surpeuplé
overlook (to) 17
  donner (sur)
overlook (to) (something) 27
  surplomber
overweight 29
  obèse

Pakistan 80
  Pakistan
Pakistani 80
  Pakistanais
palm 26
  palmier
palm-tree 26
  palmier
panel 37
  commission, jury
park 47
  jardin public
park ranger 42
  garde forestier
parking facilities 18
  parking
parking-lot (US) 62
  parking
parkway (US) 61
  avenue
pass 7
  col (montagne)
pass 55
  carte (de train) (abonnement

général)
passenger 53
passager
passport 66
passeport
path (gén.) 40
chemin
patron (pub) 31
client
pay station (US) 45
cabine téléphonique
peaceful 17
calme (adj.)
peacefulness 39
calme (nom)
peak 10
pic, sommet
peak hours 62
heures de pointe
pedestrian 48
piéton
peninsula 27
presqu'île
penthouse suite 17
suite de luxe
personnel 36
personnel (nom)
Peru 81
Pérou
Peruvian 81
Péruvien
pet 64
animal (domestique)
petrol 62
essence
Philippine (adj.) 81
Philippin
Philippines (the) 81
Philippines (les)
phone booth 45
cabine téléphonique
photocopier 38
photocopieuse
photocopying machine 38
photocopieuse
picnic area 83
aire de pique-nique
picturesque 43, 48
pittoresque
pier 25
jetée
pillar box 45
boîte aux lettres
piste 10
piste (ski alpin)
places of interest 47
lieux d'intérêt touristique
places to see 47
lieux d'intérêt touristique
plane 50
avion
plane ticket 51
billet d'avion
platform 57
quai (train)

playground 83
zone de jeux
plummet down a slope (to) 8
descendre (pente)
Poland 81
Pologne
Pole (nom) 81
Polonais
Polish (adj.) 81
Polonais
ponctuality 54
ponctualité
pool 29
piscine
port 60
port
Portugal 81
Portugal
Portuguese 81
Portugais
post office 48
poste
potholing 44
spéléologie
predict (to) 73
prévoir
presentation 37
exposé
prevention 29
prévention
prices 73
prix / tarifs
product 73
produit
professional 73
professionnel (adj.)
profit 68
bénéfice
profitable 74
rentable
program (US) 36
programme
programme 36
programme
promontory 27
promontoire
promote (to) 74
promouvoir
protect (to) 43
protéger
pub 31
bar
public bar 31
bar
public gardens 47
jardin public
public phone 45
cabine téléphonique
public transport 63
transports en commun
pudding 32
dessert
pull out of the station 57
quitter la gare (train)

purchasing power 73
pouvoir d'achat

quaint 43
pittoresque
quaint 48
pittoresque
quarantine 67
quarantaine
quarantine period 67
quarantaine
quay 60
quai (bateau)
quiet 17
calme (adj.)

R

raft (to) 40
descendre des rapides
railcar (US) 58
wagon
railcard 55
carte (de train) (abonnement général)
railroad pass (US) 55
carte (de train) (abonnement général)
railroad schedule (US) 56
indicateur
railroads (US) 55
chemins de fer
railway pass 55
carte (de train) (abonnement général)
railway schedule 56
indicateur
railway station 56
gare
railways 55
chemins de fer
rain 14
pluie
rain (to) 14
pleuvoir
rainy 14
pluvieux
ramble 43
randonnée
rambling (activité) 43
randonnée
ramparts 49
remparts
ranch 21
ranch
range (of) 71
gamme / éventail
ranger 42
garde forestier

rate 54, 73
tarif
re-route (to) (a plane) 52
dérouter (un avion)
receipts 74
recettes
recommend (to) 33
recommander
recreational tourism 75
tourisme de loisirs
recreational vehicle 61
camping-car
red-carpet treatment 37
traitement de faveur
reef 27
récif
refreshment room 55
buffet
refund (to) 74
rembourser
register (to) 18
enregistrer
registration 18
enregistrement
registration 36
inscription
registration plate 63
plaque minéralogique
regulation(s) 67
réglementation
regulations / rules 54
règlementation / règlement
rejuvenating 29
revitalisant
relax (to) 40
détendre (se)
relaxation 29
repos
reliability 53
fiabilité, sérieux
relieve (to) 29
soulager
renaissance 49
style renaissance
renowned 33
renommé / reputé
rent 21
louer
rent (to) 62
louer (véhicule)
representative 35
délégué
reputation 75
réputation
request (to) 66
exiger
require (to) (usu. passive) 66
exiger
rescue (to) 10, 61
sauver
research (uncount) 74
recherche
reservation 19, 36, 75
réservation

reserve 43
réserve
residence tax (US) 19
taxe de séjour
rest 29
repos
rest area 61
aire de repos
restaurant 33
restaurant
restriction 67
restriction
restrooms (US) 83
toilettes
revenue 75
revenu
ride a train (to) 58
voyager en train
ridge 7
crête
ring (to) 24
entourer
ring road 63
périphérique
road 63
route
road network 63
réseau routier
road regulations (US) 62
code de la route
road sign 62
panneau (signalisation)
romanesque 49
style roman
Romania, Rumania 81
Roumanie
Romanian 81
Roumain
room 17
chambre
route 53
parcours
rugged 24
déchiquetée (côte)
run 10
piste (ski alpin)
run (to) 56
circuler (train)
run a hotel (to) 16
tenir un hôtel
run a river (to) 40
descendre des rapides
run off the rails (to) 56
dérailler
run rapids (to) 40
descendre des rapides
runway 54
piste (d'envol, d'atterrissage)
rush hours (ant.: slack hours) 62
heures de pointe

S

saddle 7
col (montagne)
safety 54
sécurité
sail (to) 60
naviguer
sailing-boat 27
voilier
sample (to) 32
goûter / déguster
Saudi Arabia 77
Arabie Saoudite
Saudi Arabian 77
Saoudien
sauna 29
sauna
savings 70
économies
scenery 43
paysage
scenic 43
pittoresque
schedule 53
horaire
schedule (US) 56
horaires
screen 38
écran
scuba-dive (to) 26
plonger (avec bouteilles)
sea 26
mer
sea bathing 23
bains de mer
sea resort 27
station balnéaire
sea- front 25
front de mer
sea-crossing 60
traversée (maritime)
seafaring 60
maritime
seafood 25
fruits de mer
seashells 24
coquillages
seaside resort 27
station balnéaire
season 14, 75
saison
seat 57
place (train)
seat-belt 62
ceinture de sécurité
seaweed 23
algues
security 54
sécurité
security deposit 20
caution
secutity bond 20
caution

sejourn tax 19
taxe de séjour
self-catering 39
autonome (hébergement, vacances)
seminar 38
séminaire
Senegal 81
Sénégal
Senegalese 81
Sénégalais
serene 17
calme (adj.)
serve (to) 52
desservir
service 33
service
service provider 73
prestataire de service
service supplier 73
prestataire de service
set 22
situé
set (to be) 27
situé (être)
set meal 32
menu (à prix fixe)
set meal service 34
table d'hôte
set menu 32
menu (à prix fixe)
setting 31
cadre
Seychelles (the) 81
Seychelles (les)
Seychellois 81
Seychellois
shanty town 45
bidonville
shape (to be in) 29
forme (être en)
shellfish 24
crustacés
shells 24
coquillages
shelter (to) (from) 23
abriter (de)
shine (sun) (to) 12
briller
ship (fem.) 58
bateau
shipboard 58
bord (à)
shipping company 59
compagnie de navigation
shipwreck 60
naufrage
shopping arcade 47
galerie marchande
shopping centre 46
centre commercial
shopping mall (US) 46
centre commercial
shore 27
rivage

shore (lake) 10
rive
shore development 23
aménagement du littoral
shoreline 25
littoral
shun (to) (a country, a destination) 68
bouder (une destination)
shuttle 53
navette
shuttle 60
navette
shuttle bus 53
navette
sightseeing tour 49
visite (d'une ville)
Singapore 81
Singapour
Singaporean 81
Singapourien
situated 22
situé
situated (to be) 27
situé (être)
ski (to) 10
skier
ski area 8
domaine skiable
ski equipment 8
équipement (de ski)
ski field 8
domaine skiable
ski gear 8
équipement (de ski)
ski instructor 9
moniteur de ski
ski lift 10
remonte-pente
ski resort 11
station de ski
ski-pass 8
forfait (ski)
ski-tow 10
remonte-pente
skiing resort 11
station de ski
skilift 11
téléski
skin-dive (to) (= to snorkel) 26
plonger (sans bouteilles)
skiwear 11
vêtements de ski
skyline 47
ligne (d'horizon, des toits...)
skyscraper 47
gratte-ciel
sled (US) 9
luge (sport)
sledge 9
luge (sport)
sleigh 11
traîneau

slide projector 38
projecteur de diapositives
slope 10
pente, piste (ski alpin)
slump 69
crise
smoking area 55
zone fumeur
snow 9, 13
neige
snow (to) 13
neiger
snow cannons 7
canon (à neige)
snow conditions 8
enneigement
snow field 9
névé
snow runway 7
altipiste / altiport
snow-chains 7
chaînes (véhicule)
snowmobile 9
motoneige
snowplough 7
chasse-neige
snowshoe 10
raquette (montagne)
snowslide 7
avalanche
soar (to) 8
culminer
Somali (nom) 81
Somalien
Somalia 81
Somalie
Somalian (adj.) 81
Somalien
South Africa 77
Afrique du Sud
South African 77
Sud-Africain
spa 30
source, station thermale
spa-goer 28
curiste
spa-town 30
station thermale
Spain 78
Espagne
Spaniard (nom) 78
Espagnol
Spanish (adj.) 78
Espagnol
speciality 33
spécialité
speciality dish 33
spécialité
speed limit 62
limitation de vitesse
spelunking (US) 44
spéléologie
spending 70
dépenses

spending capacity (US) 73
  pouvoir d'achat
spitz 10
  pic
spoil (to) 70
  dégrader
sport (s) 44
  sport (s)
spring 30
  source
square 48
  place
Sri Lanka (ex-Ceylon) 81
  Sri Lanka (ex-Ceylan)
staff 36
  personnel (nom)
stage (to) 36
  organiser
stagger (to) (payment, holidays...) 70
  échelonner (paiements, vacances...)
stake 71
  enjeu
standard of living 72
  niveau de vie
standards 69
  critères
star 32
  étoile
starlit 41
  étoilé(e)
starry 41
  étoilé(e)
starter 32
  hors-d'œuvre
station 56
  gare
stifling 13
  étouffant (chaleur)
stillness 39
  calme (nom)
stopover 52
  escale
storm 14
  tempête
stream 11
  torrent
street 49
  rue
stretch 24
  étendue (nom)
stretch (to) 8
  étendre (s')
stroll (to) 46
  flâner
subside (to) 12
  calmer (se) (vent, tempête...)
subsidies 75
  subventions
suburban lines 56
  lignes de banlieue
subway (US) 57
  métro

Sudan (the) 81
  Soudan
Sudanese 81
  Soudanais
suite 17
  suite
sultry 13
  étouffant (chaleur)
summit 10
  sommet
sun 14, 27
  soleil
sunbathe (to) 23
  bronzer
sunny 24
  ensoleillé
sunny spell 13
  éclaircie
sunshine 27
  soleil
surf 23
  brisants
surround (to) 24
  entourer
Swede (nom) 81
  Suédois
Sweden 81
  Suède
Swedish (adj.) 81
  Suédois
sweltering 13
  étouffant (chaleur)
Swiss 81
  Suisse
Switzerland 81
  Suisse
symposium 38
  symposium (pl.: symposia)
Syria 81
  Syrie
Syrian 81
  Syrien

T

T-bar 11
  téléski
tab (US) 31
  addition
table d'hôte 34
  table d'hôte
table d'hôte menu 32
  menu (à prix fixe)
tailback 62
  embouteillage
tailor-made 75
  sur-mesure, à la carte
take a hike (to) 42
  marcher
take a walk (to) 42
  marcher
take to do something 42
  mettre à (se) (+ activité)

take off (to) 51
  décoller
take place (to) 36
  lieu (avoir)
take place (to) (at, in) 47
  lieu (avoir)
take to something (to) 42
  mettre à (se) (+ activité)
take to the slopes (to) 10
  skier
tape-recorder 38
  magnétophone
target 69
  cible
taste (to) 32
  goûter / déguster
tax 75
  taxe
tax-free airport shop 51
  boutique hors-taxe
taxi 63
  taxi
taxi (to) 54
  rouler (avion)
taxicab 63
  taxi
tea-shop 33
  salon de thé
temperate 14
  tempéré
temperature 14
  température
terminal 50
  aérogare
Thai 81
  Thaïlandais
Thailand 81
  Thaïlande
thatched cottage 20
  chaumière
theater (US) 49
  théâtre
theatre 49
  théâtre
theme park 73
  parc à thème
therapeutic 30
  thérapeutique (adj.)
therapy 30
  thérapie
thermae 30
  thermes
thermal 30
  thermal
thermal cure 28
  cure
thermal resort 30
  station thermale
thriving 71
  florissant
throng 42
  foule
thunderstorm 14
  orage

Tibet 81
Tibet
Tibetan 81
Tibétain
ticket 54
titre de transport
ticket 55
billet
ticket (US) 61
amende
ticket booth 45
bureau de location (théâtre, spectacles)
ticket office 45
bureau de location (théâtre, spectacles)
ticket office 56
guichet
ticket-collector 56
contrôleur
ticketing 68
billeterie
tide 25
marée
tie up (to) 58
amarrer
time-sharing 21
multi-propriété
time-zone 53
fuseau horaire
timetable 56
horaires
tip 32
pourboire
toboggan 9
luge (sport)
toilets 83
toilettes
toll 63
péage
toll-free number 19
numéro vert
top 10
sommet
top (to) 70
dépasser / excéder
touch down (to) 50
atterrir
tour 40
circuit
tour 49
visite (d'une ville)
tour book (US) 47
guide touristique
tour escort 68
accompagnateur
tour leader 68
accompagnateur
touring guide 47
guide touristique
Tourism Office, Convention and Visitors Bureau 48
office de tourisme
tourist attendance 71
fréquentation (touristique)

Tourist Board 48
office de tourisme
tourist class hotel 16
hôtel classe touriste
tourist information centre 49
syndicat d'initiative
tourist policy 73
politique touristique
tow 10
remonte-pente
tower (to) 8
culminer
town 49
ville
town hall 47
hôtel de ville
town twinning 72
jumelage (ville)
town-planning 49
urbanisme
trade-fair 36
salon (foire, exposition)
traffic 62
circulation
traffic-jam 62
embouteillage
trail 44
sentier
trailer (US) 61
caravane
train 57
train
training 71
formation
tranquil 17
calme (adj.)
transfer 54
transfert
travel agency 68
agence de voyages
travel by train (to) 58
voyager en train
travel data 70
documentation touristique
travel literature 70
documentation touristique
traveler's checks (US) 64
chèques de voyage
traveller's cheques 64
chèques de voyage
travelogue 70
documentaire (de voyage)
treatment 30
traitement
trek (to) 44
faire du trekking
trekking 44
trekking
trend 42
mode
trim (to be in) 29
forme (être en)
trip 76
voyage

try (to) 32
goûter / déguster
Tube (the) (London) 57
métro
Tunisia 82
Tunisie
Tunisian 82
Tunisien
turbulence (uncount) 55
turbulence
Turk (nom) 82
Turc (nom)
Turkey 82
Turquie
Turkish (adj.) 82
Turque (adj.)
turnover 69
chiffre d'affaires
twilight 12
crépuscule
twinkle (stars) (to) 12
briller
typhoon 14
typhon

U

U.S.A. (United States of America) 78
Etats-Unis
umbrella 26
parasol
undergroud 57
métro
underpass 63
périphérique
underwater 27
sous-marin (adj.)
university 49
université
unlimited 34
volonté (à)
unlimited mileage 62
kilométrage illimité
unspoiled 27
vierge (intact, pas défiguré)
unspoilt 27
vierge (intact, pas défiguré)
unusual holidays 44
vacances originales
unwind (to) 40
détendre (se)
Uruguay 82
Uruguay
Uruguayan 82
Uruguayen

V

V.A.T. (value added tax) 34
T.V.A.

LEXIQUE ANGLAIS

vacancies 19
  libre (chambre)
vacancy 19
  libre (chambre)
vacate (to) (a room) 19
  libérer (une chambre)
vacations (US) 76
  vacances
vaccination 67
  vaccination
valley 11
  vallée
van 61
  camping-car
Venezuela 82
  Vénézuela
Venezuelan 82
  Vénézuelien
venue 36
  lieu
**video-cassette-recorder
(VCR)** 38
  magnétoscope
Vietnam 82
  Vietnam
Vietnamese 82
  Vietnamien
viewing area 83
  point de vue
visa 67
  visa
**visitor information center
(US)** 49
  syndicat d'initiative
vista 48
  panorama, point de vue
volcano (pl.: volcanoes) 11
  volcan
voucher 18
  bon d'échange / bon de
  paiement
voyage 60
  traversée (maritime)

voyage 76
  voyage

waiter(ress) 33
  serveur(euse)
waiting-room 57
  salle d'attente
walk (to) 42
  marcher
wall 9
  paroi (rocheuse)
walls 49
  remparts
warmth 12
  chaleur
watch (to) 43
  observer
waterfront 25
  front de mer
watersports 27
  sports nautiques
wave 27
  vague
weather 14
  temps
**well-appointed / well
equipped, appointed (with) /
equipped (with)** 17
  bien-aménagé / bien- equipé
well-known 33
  renommé / reputé
wet 13
  humide
wharf (pl.: wharves) 60
  quai (bateau)
wheel-chair access 18
  aménagements pour les
  handicapés
"white stuff" 9
  neige

wildlife 41
  faune
wildlife park 43
  réserve
wind 15, 27
  vent
window-shopping 47
  lèche-vitrine
**wine (white, sparkling, rosé,
red...)** 34
  vin (blanc, pétillant, rosé,
  rouge...)
wine and dine (to) (someone) 32
  inviter (quelqu'un au
  restaurant)
wine route 43
  route des vins
wine-waiter 33
  sommelier
winter resort 11
  station de ski
winter sports 11
  sports d'hiver
word processor 38
  machine à traitement de
  texte
workshop 37
  atelier

youth hostel 20
  auberge de jeunesse
Yugoslav (nom) 82
  Yougoslave
Yugoslavia 82
  Yougoslavie
Yugoslavian (adj.) 82
  Yougoslave
Zaire 82
  Zaïre
Zairean 82
  Zaïrois

Aubin Imprimeur
LIGUGÉ, POITIERS

Achevé d'imprimer en janvier 1993
N° d'impression L 42032
Dépôt légal janvier 1993
Imprimé en France